COMPLETE STEP-BY-STEP
Upholstery

COMPLETE STEP-BY-STEP
Upholstery

DAVID SOWLE and **RUTH DYE**

First published in 2005 by
New Holland Publishers (UK) Ltd
This edition published in 2005 by Struik Publishers
(a division of New Holland (South Africa) (Pty) Ltd)
New Holland Publishers is a member of Johnnic Communications Ltd
80 McKenzie Street
Cape Town 8001
South Africa
www.struik.co.za

Garfield House
86–88 Edgware Road
London
W2 2EA
United Kingdom

14 Aquatic Drive
Frenchs Forest, NSW 2086
Australia

218 Lake Road
Northcote, Auckland
New Zealand

Copyright © 2005 text: David Sowle and Ruth Dye
Copyright © 2005 photographs: New Holland Publishers (UK) Ltd
Copyright © 2005 New Holland Publishers (UK) Ltd

David Sowle and Ruth Dye have asserted their moral right
to be identified as the authors of this work.

All rights reserved. No part of this publication may be
reproduced, stored in a retrieval system, or transmitted in
any form or by any means, electronic, mechanical,
photocopying, recording or otherwise, without the prior
written permission of the publishers and copyright holders.

ISBN 1 77007 156 3

Senior Editor: Clare Hubbard
Editorial Direction: Rosemary Wilkinson
Step-by-step photographs: David Sowle
Finished projects and close-ups: Shona Wood
Design: Peter Crump
Illustrations: Stephen Dew
Location: pp 51, 75, 83, 91, 117, 141 www.lightlocations.co.uk
Location: pp 35, 43, 59, 67, 101, 109, 149 www.1st-option.net
Production: Hazel Kirkman

1 3 5 7 9 10 8 6 4 2

Reproduction by Modern Age Repro House Ltd, Hong Kong
Printed and bound by Times Offset (M) Sdn. Bhd., Malaysia

Note
The author and publishers have made every effort to ensure
that all instructions given in this book are safe and accurate,
but they cannot accept liability for any resulting injury or loss
or damage to either property or person, whether direct or
consequential and howsoever arising.

contents

INTRODUCTION 6
GETTING STARTED 8
BASIC UPHOLSTERY TECHNIQUES 14

BASIC SKILLS 32

1. Drop-in seat 34
2. Pin-cushion seat 42
3. Overstuffed seat 50
4. Overstuffed chair with springs 58
5. Deep-buttoned stool 66
6. Caning 74
7. Box cushion 82
8. Re-covering upholstery 90

APPLYING BASIC SKILLS 98

9. Art Deco armchair 100
10. Classic armchair 108
11. Wing chair 116
12. Tub chair 124
13. Chaise longue 132
14. Drop-arm sofa 140
15. Buttoned leather chesterfield 148

Glossary 156
Suppliers 157
Index 159

Introduction

If you want to learn upholstery all you need is a book, some basic tools and a chair. That's how we began, and this is the book we wish we'd had.

Our upholstery business started when Ruth decided she wanted to have a go at upholstering a chair. I went over the road to a friend who had an antiques shop and asked if Ruth could have a chair, and we hunted around local junk shops for secondhand tools. Our friend gave me an old oak carver and a Victorian nursing chair from the basement and said Ruth could do what she liked with them. It seemed to take days just to strip them, but finally they were both clean of their old upholstery. Ruth asked another friend, who made cushions and curtains, to order some materials from her supplier and slowly, by following the instructions in an old upholstery book and plenty of trial and error, Ruth reupholstered the two chairs. Neither could be described as fine examples, but, our friend was more than happy to put them in his shop and when they sold – as they both did – he split the proceeds with us.

From then on he supplied as much upholstery work as Ruth could handle. Small things at first, but many and varied – boxes, piano stools, fire surrounds with cushion tops – anything bought cheap at auction and in need of upholstery. If the finished article sold in his shop – and they all did sooner or later – he shared the profits with us.

Soon Ruth had enough work and confidence in her upholstery skills to give up her day job. We couldn't afford to rent or buy a shop, so we began offering our furniture through our website at www.oldsofas.com. We now reupholster and sell old sofas and chairs to customers all over the UK and Europe.

This book is full of step-by-step photographs, taken in real time, of Ruth upholstering 15 different pieces in our workshop. To that we've added advice on Getting Started – what tools and materials to buy, where to find furniture and what to look for – all the things you need to know before you embark on your first project. This is followed by a section on Basic Upholstery Techniques, in which we've covered areas that we haven't been able to mention in conjunction with the projects, or ones we felt needed a little more explanation than the reference in the projects allowed. Stripping furniture, webbing, tying springs, knots, stuffing, regulating, edge roll stitching, hand stitching, buying fabric, making cutting plans, making single and double piping and cushion inners are all included in this section. For those of you on upholstery courses we've even included the Van Dyke join. This is the part of the book to return to if you're unsure of the basics at any point.

We've divided the 15 upholstery projects into two sections: Basic Skills and Applying Basic Skills. Basic Skills comprises eight upholstery projects that introduce and teach you all the basic skills that must be mastered in order to progress to more complex projects.

The first three projects use simple, inexpensive chairs to illustrate the three most common upholstery methods; stuffed pad, pin-cushion and overstuffed. Project 4 – Overstuffed chair with springs – introduces springs to an upholstered seat, and project 5 – Deep-buttoned stool – shows you how to put deep buttons into upholstery. Project 6 – Caning – shows you how to cane; a skill that all well-rounded upholsterers should have; and project 7 – Box cushion – demonstrates the principles and practice of how to make piped, removable outer cushion covers. The last of the basic skills projects, project 8 – Re-covering upholstery – rounds things off with a detailed explanation of how to do a re-covering job.

The Applying Basic Skills section takes the skills learnt in the previous eight projects and applies them to seven more advanced projects. Culminating in a sumptuous buttoned leather chesterfield, the projects in this section all offer something to add to the basic skills, but demonstrate that any upholstery project, no matter what the piece is, breaks down into the application of one or more of the basic skills.

Project 9 – Art Deco armchair – introduces more complex seat springing and arm covering techniques and project 10 – Classic armchair – explains sprung arms and finishing scrolls. Project 11 shows how to upholster a chair with wings and project 12 is a masterclass on dealing with curves explaining how to upholster a beautiful tub chair. Project 13 takes the buttoning skills learnt in project 5 and expands and applies them to a fabulous Victorian chaise longue. Project 14 gives a detailed explanation on how to upholster a sofa with a drop arm and project 15 combines leather, deep buttons and curves with the classic Victorian chesterfield.

None of the 15 projects in this book should be looked at in terms of difficulty. Project 1 – Drop-in seat – takes a lot less time and work to complete than project 15 – Buttoned leather chesterfield – but that doesn't mean it is easier. You will certainly need to know how to perform more upholstery operations to complete a chesterfield, but bad upholstery looks bad whether it's on a pin-cushion seat in a junk shop window or on a Louis XV chaise in a museum.

Reupholstering old furniture combines good old-fashioned craftsmanship with modern aspirations to recycle. It takes time to build the confidence necessary to take on the more complex projects, but with practice, and a little help from this book, your results will soon be every bit as good as the professionals. Take pride in all the pieces you upholster and enjoy yourself.

Getting started

Before you can make a start on your first upholstery project there are three things you need to acquire: tools, materials and a piece of furniture.

Tools

These can be divided crudely into two categories: upholstery tools that you'll have to buy, and general tools that you probably have already. The golden rule for any tool is that good ones will perform well and last a lifetime, so buy the best you can afford. Whenever you're out searching second-hand shops and auctions for reupholstery bargains, search for tools as well: fine-quality tools can be bought for a fraction of their brand-new cost.

A basic upholstery tool kit comprises: wooden mallet, magnetic tack hammer, webbing stretcher, tack lifter, 13 cm (5 in) spring needle, 30 cm (12 in) double-ended needle and 25 cm (10 in) stuffing regulator.

Wooden mallet: this is used mainly when stripping, to hammer the tack lifter when removing old tacks and staples. There is no need to spend too much money – a normal carpenter's beech mallet will do. Soak it in linseed oil for 24 hours before you use it for the first time and you'll never need to buy another one.

Magnetic tack hammer: an essential upholstery tool. One end of the head is magnetic and acts like a third hand. If you sprinkle some tacks in a small container, you can pick them up, one at a time, with the magnetic end, then tack and hammer home while holding the material in place with your free hand. You can buy expensive bronze-headed versions, but in this case the cheaper ones work just as well.

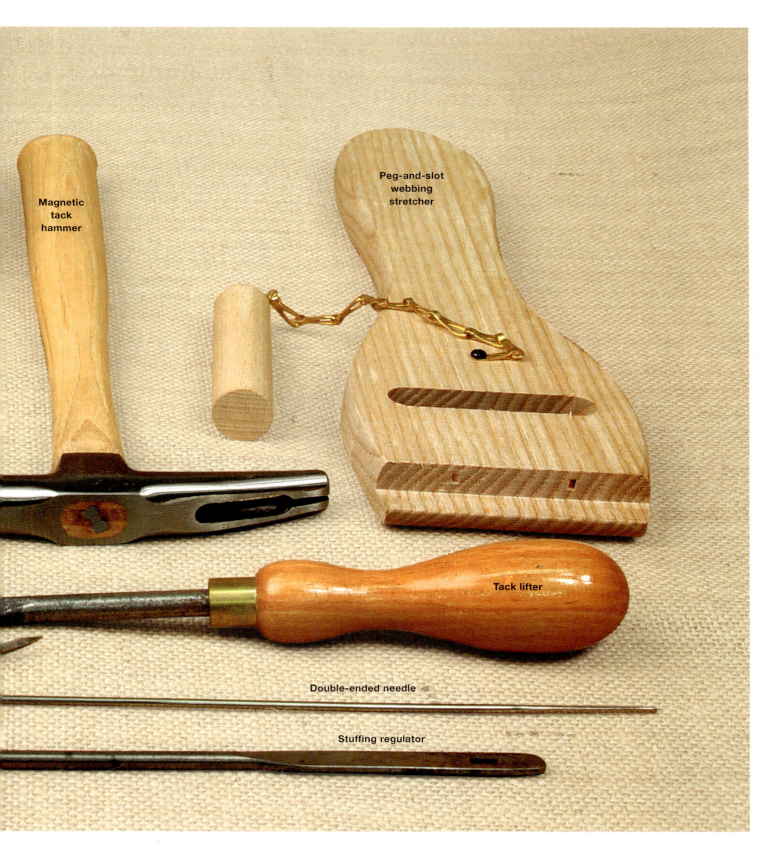

GETTING STARTED 9

Magnetic tack hammers

Webbing pliers

Peg-and-slot webbing stretcher

Webbing stretcher: this is used to tension the webbing in a seat base tighter than you can using your hands alone (see page 16). They come in various styles, but all use some method or other to grip the webbing and lever against the seat frame to achieve the required tension.

The peg-and-slot version is the least expensive but it is a little slow to use because the webbing needs to be passed through the slot and held by the peg (see photo bottom left). Soak it in linseed oil for 24 hours before you use it for the first time and you'll never need to replace it.

Tack lifter: used for removing old tacks and staples during stripping, tack lifters come in various shapes, but are all designed to lever out tacks. Loose tacks can be levered out manually, but generally the tack lifter is designed to be hammered with a wooden mallet. You don't have to spend a lot of money on a tack lifter but, as with all tools, you get what you pay for. Our advice is to buy a good one because you'll be using it over and over again.

Needles: the spring needle and double-ended needle are used for stitching with various upholstery twines. The former is for sewing springs to webbing and hessian, and for sewing stuffing ties. The latter is for stitching edge rolls, sewing through stuffing ties and for buttoning.

Upholstery skewers: small, bright metal skewers with a loop end and point. Usually 10 cm (4 in) and 7.5 cm (3 in) long, they are used in upholstery applications instead of pins to hold hessian, calico and fabric in place, usually while they are being positioned ready to hand stitch.

Stuffing regulator: this is a strong, thick needle, rather like a knitting needle, with either a flat end or plastic handle. When you cover fibre or horsehair stuffing with hessian or calico, you'll usually find that the stuffing needs to be distributed more evenly, moved up to make a firmer edge or pushed into corners. This is done by using a stuffing regulator to lever the fibre inside the pad to wherever you want it.

Other tools: in addition to these specialist upholstery tools, you will need a pair of scissors, a tape measure, pincers, a knife and needles for hand stitching.

Sewing machines: most of the projects in this book can be completed without a sewing machine. However, there are some jobs – making cushions and piping, for example – that are impractical without one. For a handful of projects a year, a domestic sewing machine should be perfectly adequate. If you are likely to sew heavy upholstery fabrics on a more regular basis however, you really ought to consider investing in an industrial machine – one that will cope easily with leather and other heavy fabrics.

Materials

Traditionally upholstered furniture consists of a strong wooden frame, supplemented and filled in with webbing, which then supports individual springs. Layers of hessian and calico are placed over the top of the springs and frame, with one or two layers of stuffing – usually in the form of vegetable fibre or

GETTING STARTED 11

horsehair – sandwiched between them. Finally, a layer of wadding is laid over the upholstery and covered by the top fabric. All of the elements that make up the upholstery are variously stitched, tied and nailed to each other and the frame using twine, cord and tacks.

Modern upholstered furniture is made of a less substantial wooden frame, which is supplemented and filled in with plywood and cardboard, and padded with man-made foam sheets and edgings of varying thickness, shape and density. If webbing is used, it is made of rubber. Finally, a layer of synthetic fleece is laid over the padding and covered by the top fabric. Glue and staples are used to attach the materials and fabric to each other and the frame.

Webbing: this comprises a series of tightly woven strips in varying widths – from 5–10 cm (2–4 in) – made of cotton, flax, jute, or a mixture of two.

Vegetable fibre: this is black or ginger, hair-like fibre made from coconut husks or other vegetable stalks. All vegetable fibre manufactured for use in upholstery will have been treated to make it fire retardant.

Horsehair: a traditional stuffing, this can be washed and reused if found when stripping old upholstery, though only good-quality, long, curly hair is worth saving. Wild boar hair can be used as a modern substitute.

Hessian: a thick, strong material that comes in various weights from 200–400 g (7–16 oz). The strongest, or heaviest, is often called tarpaulin. Don't get too concerned with using different weights for different jobs, just buy a strong, quality hessian that you like working with and stick with it.

Calico: a strong, cotton cloth, usually bleached, used as a final layer over the top of stuffing before the application of wadding and top fabric. Sometimes a black version is used for bottom cloths. It is available in various weights, and 140 g (5 oz) is fine for most upholstery applications.

Wadding: this comes in sheets 2.5 cm (1 in) thick, but can be peeled apart to half thickness. It is used as a final, smooth layer on top of the coarser stuffing, underneath the top fabric.

Synthetic fleece: a fine, light, manmade fleece 12 mm (½ in) thick which comes in huge expanded rolls. It adds nothing to the padding of the upholstery but is used as a thin layer between the cotton wadding and top fabric to stop the wadding from sticking to the back of the fabric.

Twine: there are various types available. Flax twine comes in different thicknesses, usually denoted by a number. No.1 is the thickest and is used for tying springs to webbing and hessian. Nos. 2 and 3 are thinner and used for stitching edge rolls and stuffing ties. Buttoning twine is made of nylon and can be used as an alternative to flax twine. It's extremely strong and so best used for buttoning.

Lay cord: this is a thick cord made from jute or hemp and is used for tying springs together.

Tacks: upholstery tacks must be used for upholstery; other varieties of tack and nail are not suitable and can damage wooden frames. They come in sizes from 10–20 mm (⅜–¾ in) and two varieties of each: improved tacks have larger heads than fine tacks. As a guide use 20 mm (¾ in) improved tacks for attaching lay cord and webbing, 13 mm (½ in) improved tacks for hessian, calico and top fabric, and 10 mm (⅜ in) fine tacks for scrolls and finer work.

Netting staples: sometimes used to secure springs to the wood on the top of arms and the front edge of seats. We generally hold springs in place by attaching a length of webbing over their bases, but sometimes it's easier to use netting staples. Ordinary galvanized netting staples are used; there's no upholstery equivalent.

Tacking strip: a 12 mm (½ in) wide strip of strong card that comes in rolls and is used most commonly to invisibly attach the outside arm fabric to the underside of an arm or wherever else an invisible join is required. The tacking strip is laid over the underside of the fabric and tacked in place so that it forms a smooth, straight edge when the fabric is pulled over it. You often find tacking strips improvised from bits of cereal packets.

Upholstered furniture: what to buy and where

Being a good upholsterer and buying the right furniture to upholster are two different skills. We have been buying upholstered furniture for many years and yet we still occasionally pay good money for pieces that turn out to be bad buys. There's an overlap between the two skills: the better you are at buying furniture, the easier it will be to turn it into something you are proud of. Whatever your upholstery ambitions, your best starting point is to get out there and train your eye to spot a bargain.

Start close to home: if you're new to upholstery your confidence will be fortified if you start with small, uncomplicated projects: the sorts of pieces you probably have already – dining chairs or a piano stool, for example. If you don't have anything yourself, the chances are there'll be auntie's old chair in a relative's loft somewhere. Beg, borrow or steal from your family before you go out and buy anything to work on.

Antiques shops: these are great places for rummaging through, but not necessarily to buy from. There's nothing wrong with buying the odd dining chair if it costs only a few pounds, but a piece with any value will have been tidied up for the sale and will most likely look better than it actually is. Use these shops with a view to learning and training your eye. Price tickets often carry information regarding the age and style of a piece and will give you an idea of relative value. Spend as much time as possible wandering around musty old buildings, turning over price tags, and pay special attention to pieces that have been newly upholstered. Dealers will get their upholstery done as cheaply as possible and so the result is usually more show than substance – well worth a good look with a critical eye.

Auctions: house-clearance auctions are the upholsterer's Aladdin's cave. Most reasonably sized towns will have at least one auction house – very often run by a local estate agent – where, once or twice a month, sales of house contents and other general items are held. There will be a time, usually the day before or on the morning of the sale, when you can view all the items for sale and decide if there's anything you might want to buy.

When you arrive at a viewing you will find an area filled with rows of wardrobes, book shelves, old pianos, dressers, tables and all manner of old and modern household items. In the middle of the room, usually facing the auctioneer's podium, will be rows and rows of dining chairs, armchairs and sofas. Each piece or set of pieces will be given a lot number. The bigger, more organized, auction houses will issue a catalogue or a printed list of items for sale, giving the lot number and a brief description of what, in the auctioneer's opinion, it is, and how much they suggest it might sell for. For example: "Lot 269 – a late-Victorian elbow chair with turned legs and bobbin stretchers, £30–£40." Auctioneers generally have years of experience and are, therefore, very authoritative on what something is. This makes the auction catalogue an excellent tool for learning about the age, era and features of different chairs and sofas.

Make a note of the lot number of anything you might want to buy, go to the auction office and ask how you bid, what time the auction starts and how many lots they get through in an hour. You'll probably be asked for your name and address and be given a card with a number on it: this is the number the auctioneer will write against any lots that you buy so he knows who's bought what. On the day of the auction make sure you arrive in good time for the lot numbers on which you intend to bid. This way you can get a feel for how the auctioneer works. You will probably be asked to pay for and remove anything you buy on the day, so make sure you have an acceptable method of payment – usually cash – and adequate transport.

Don't be intimidated by bidding. When the auctioneer calls out the lot number, an assistant will indicate the piece it relates to and the auctioneer will confirm the piece's description and put forward a starting price. If no one bids, the price will be lowered until someone does or until the auctioneer moves on to the next lot. Make sure you can be seen by the auctioneer and, when you want to bid, attract his or her attention by waving your bidding number. Once the auctioneer knows you are bidding he or she will check to see if you want to keep up with the sale. Simply indicate whether you wish to continue or not. If you are the last bidder when the auctioneer sells the lot, he or she will want to know your bidding number. It will take a little time for the office to know who has bought what, so wait a little before going to pay. Once you've paid, auction staff will help you remove your lots.

AUCTION TIPS

Use the viewing at an auction as an opportunity to have a thorough look at anything you find interesting, whether you intend to buy it or not: auctions are one of the few places where you can prod and poke old pieces of furniture with impunity. Here are some things to consider when viewing any sofa or chair that you think you might buy:

1. Start with the wood. Pay attention to the legs first: unless you're a carpenter you won't be able to fix broken ones, and the same applies to any show wood. Also, legs and show wood can tell you whether something is genuinely old or just looks it.

2. Look out for signs of woodworm. Often the beetles eat just the soft wood dowels that hold the frame together, or concentrate in one area of the frame, leaving the rest untouched. It can be treated with a woodworm killer.

3. Look carefully at the piece from all angles and compare reference points on each side to see if it looks symmetrical. Weird and wonderful is fine, but don't buy anything that strikes you as having an odd shape, or just not quite right. One missing castor is a warning sign: if the piece has been used in that condition, undue stress will have been put on the frame and as a result will probably need repairs.

4. Don't pre-judge a piece because it has a nasty flowery slip (loose) cover. From experience, wonderful old sofas and chairs are sometimes disguised under such covers in an effort to prolong the life of something that has gone out of fashion.

5. Don't worry about the upholstery. The condition of the upholstery is only relevant as far as it goes to confirm or dispel your opinions about the age of the piece. Feel underneath: if there is webbing and springs, the piece is probably pre-1950; if not it's likely to be more modern.

6. Target anything that cannot be used in its present condition. Dealers won't buy pieces that they need to spend money on, and most people won't buy things that have to be reupholstered before they can use them, leaving you to pick up a bargain.

Basic upholstery techniques

This section covers the basic skills that apply to many upholstery projects: including stripping furniture, attaching webbing, tying knots, hand stitching, making piping and cushion inners, measuring up and making a cutting plan, and how to do a Van Dyke join. The only way to learn is by experience: together with additional techniques in the projects that follow, this section will equip you with all you need to take on any upholstery challenge with absolute confidence.

Stripping furniture

The object of the stripping process is to remove all existing upholstery so that you are left with the bare wooden frame. Unless, of course, you only want to re-cover the piece, as you might with modern foam-filled furniture, in which case you'll stop stripping once the top cover is off. There is no right or

wrong way to do this: as long as you avoid damaging the show wood, the frame and, more importantly, yourself, it's up to you. Here's a guide as to what tools you'll need and a few things to help you get started.

Tools for stripping: there are many specialist stripping tools – ripping chisels, ripping hammers and specialist knives – but all you are likely to need are a tack lifter, a wooden mallet, scissors, a knife and pincers.

Before you start: although there is no secret formula, there are a few things that you need to think about before, and while, you're stripping, which might make reupholstering the piece a little easier. Have a good look at the chair or sofa and think about how you're going to reupholster it. You'll want to measure up for the top fabric (see page 28) while the piece still has some shape so take a good look before you remove anything. Is it a piece that you're familiar with or does it have any idiosyncrasies that will potentially cause you problems? If so, how has it been upholstered? Has it been done well or badly? It is best to ask such questions before you dive in. If this is the first time you are upholstering a particular style of furniture, you will learn all you need to know for reupholstering by stripping it carefully. Make notes and sketches, or take photographs, if there's something you'll need to remember – button positions for example, or a rosette on the scroll of a chaise. Weeks from now, when you're faced with a bare frame and a box of springs you'll be glad you did.

Getting started: how you start depends on whether you're faced with a drop-in seat pad or a drop-arm sofa, but the tools and techniques employed are essentially the same. The bottom cloth is invariably the best place to start, so turn the piece over and, using a tack or staple lifter, start removing the tacks or staples holding it on (see right).

Staples can sometimes be removed by hand, but generally you'll remove tacks by butting the tack lifter up against the tack head and hammering the tack lifter with a mallet while levering upwards. Once the bottom cloth is off you'll have access to the tacks that secure the top fabric, the hessian and webbing. The mallet and tack lifter will do most of the work, but you'll need scissors and a knife to cut stitches, twine and lay cord, and a pair of pincers to remove stubborn tacks and staples. Keep going and use the stripping process to see how to put the upholstery back together again.

What to save: the only elements of the existing upholstery you'll want to reuse (assuming they are in good condition) are the springs, the horsehair and the cane from the front-edge springs. Everything else should be discarded. Don't concern yourself with broken, fractured or badly buckled springs: they will have to be replaced. A good squash between your hands will tell you if they're good or not. If the chair or sofa has front-edge springs, save the cane or wire that runs along the top of them. Leave the springs attached as a reminder of which ones to use along the front edge. Good-quality horsehair, which is curly with an element of spring, can be reused. Stuff it into pillowcases, tie the tops and machine wash. Add a little fabric conditioner to the wash and you'll find the horsehair easier to handle once dried.

> **SAFETY**
>
> Tools used for stripping have the potential to cause harm. Direct sharp tools away from you. Make sure the piece you're working on is well supported and cannot move around. This isn't likely to be a problem with a sofa, but a drop-in seat or small chair will need to be supported on a bench or on trestles. Always use disposable particle masks when stripping furniture to protect your nose and lungs from the dust that accumulates in a 100-year-old sofa.

Webbing

Webbing is the foundation of all traditional upholstery. Not only does it form a firm, elastic base for springs, stuffing and all the upholstery that goes on top, but it also pulls the wood frame together so that it becomes a strong, weight-bearing structure. Webbing a seat base is the first upholstery step in all but one of the projects in this book and requires the use of a webbing stretcher. The process of applying webbing to the seat base is the same, irrespective of the size, shape or style of furniture you're upholstering. As a general rule, seats without springs are webbed on top of the frame and seats with springs are webbed underneath.

1. Attach one end of the webbing to the back of the seat frame and run it across to the front, making sure you have enough over to fold each end back on itself. Apply tension to the webbing by using a webbing stretcher or pliers to hold the opposite end of the webbing while you attach it to the seat frame. The best way to attach each end of webbing is as follows, using five 16 mm (⅝ in) tacks: hammer one tack in at each edge and one in the centre. Fold the end of the webbing over and hammer a tack either side of the centre one.

2. Once you've attached all the webbing running from back to front, repeat the process, attaching webbing running from side to side, weaving in and out alternately as you go.

Tying seat springs

The function of springs in upholstery is not to pad, but to return a seat, arm or back to its original position once the sitter has stood up. Seat springs have weight to support and need to be held in position securely within the upholstery so they don't move around and, over time, break free. Seat springs are tied using lay cord so that they act in unison, like a mattress, and stay in position during many years of hard use. Arm and back springs are often tied together as well, but this is not so important and has as much to do with holding them in position during the upholstery process as getting them to work together. Tying seat springs is carried out once they have been stitched in place on top of the seat webbing (see step 4, project 4, page 61 for details).

1. Hammer a 20 mm (¾ in) tack into the top of the seat rail opposite each edge spring so that 7 mm (¼ in) of each tack is protruding. Cut lengths of lay cord for each row of springs: for example nine springs in a box shape consists of three rows of springs running front to back and three rows of springs running side to side and so will require six lengths of lay cord. Tie one end of the lay cord to one of the 20 mm (¾ in) tacks and using a clove hitch (see page 18) tie it halfway up the first spring in the row and then each subsequent spring in the row until you reach the opposite seat rail. Tie this end of the lay cord to the top of the tack at the end of that row. Keep the lay cord tight and tension the springs as you go.

Repeat until all springs are tied halfway up front to back and side to side. Hammer the tacks home to secure the cord.

2. Repeat the above, but this time cut longer lengths of lay cord and tie them to the tacks with 20 cm (8 in) spare cord at each end. Tie to the second loop down of the first spring, over the tops of each subsequent spring, and to the second loop down of the last spring. Tie the cord to the tack at that end with 20 cm (8 in) spare. Use each 20 cm (8 in) spare length to tie the top spring loop of each end spring.

Chairs with small seats, like the Overstuffed chair with springs in project 4 (see pages 60–65), need only be tied over the top of the springs. Chairs with substantial seats and all sofas should be tied over the top and half way up as described above in steps 1 and 2.

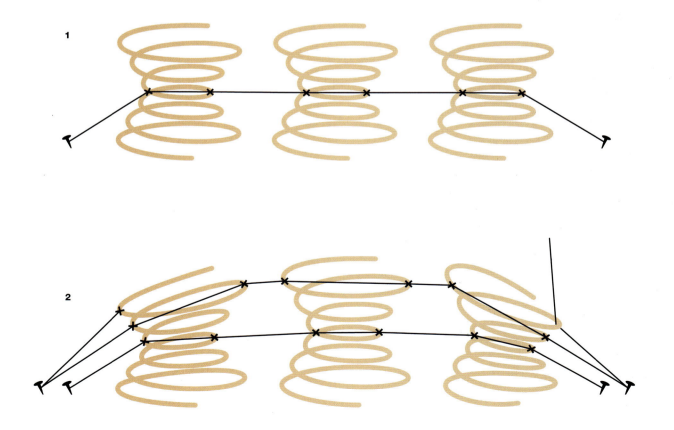

Knots

Surprisingly, you need to know just two knots for upholstery. The first is the clove hitch, which is used for tying springs, and the other is a slipknot, which is used just about everywhere else, most notably when tying buttons.

Clove hitch

First take the cord over the spring from back to front and around to the left-hand side, behind the loose end. Then take the cord over the spring, again from front to back and through the loop you have made.

Slipknot

1. Take a length of twine, make a loop at one end and hold it between your thumb and forefinger.

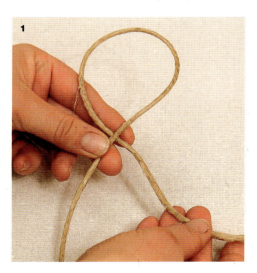

2. Take the cut end of twine and wrap it loosely once around the loop you are holding.

3. Repeat, and, holding the loops in place, pass the end of the twine through the first loop, from back to front, down through the middle of the two loops wrapped around the thumb and out at the bottom.

4. The finished knot. Use a slipknot when buttoning and for starting a line of ties, whipping or stitches.

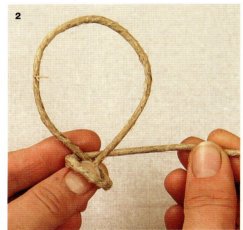

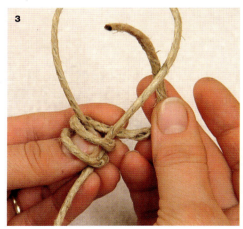

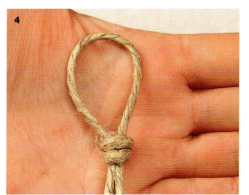

Whipping cane to seat edge springs

Attach cane to the top of the springs along the front edge of a seat by lashing, or whipping, it with flax twine. Whipping is easy to do, but can be very tough on your hands, especially if you've got 12 springs to secure along the front of a three-seater sofa. Buy some sticking plasters and wrap one or two around the parts of your fingers that grip the twine.

1. Start by securing the twine around the spring top and cane, using a slipknot. Pass the twine over the top of the cane, from front to back, while holding a loop of twine at the front, then pass the twine through the loop and pull up tight.

2. Repeat the whipping process until the cane is held by 2.5 cm (1 in) or more of lashing and then tie it off.

Stuffing

The padding in traditional upholstery is supplied by a stuffing of one or more fibrous materials. Most people think that all old furniture is full of horsehair, and it's true that horsehair was a popular stuffing in furniture, mattresses and other upholstery manufactured during the Victorian times (1837–1901) and earlier. Often, however, and certainly since Edwardian times (1901–1910), most upholstered furniture was stuffed with a combination of vegetable fibre and horsehair, or vegetable fibre alone.

All upholstery, except for the thinnest of upholstered pads, requires two separate stuffings. The first should constitute 80 per cent of the overall padding and the second a smoothing-over layer to cover up lumps and bumps on the surface of the first layer, usually caused by through-stuffing ties and the like. If you are going to use horsehair, use it for the second stuffing only.

Stuffing ties

Stuffing ties are loose loops of flax or buttoning twine stitched over the surface of hessian to hold the stuffing in place.

1. Start with a slipknot and sew large, evenly-spaced stitches in rows to cover the whole area of the hessian.

2. Tuck a handful of stuffing under each of the stuffing ties, forming an even covering over the whole area.

Regulating the stuffing

A stuffing regulator is used to distribute stuffing more evenly once it's inside a covering. Regulating should be carried out after every stuffing and in between rows of edge-roll stitches.

1. Use one hand to feel for lumps and irregularities in the stuffing.

2. With a stuffing regulator, use the other hand to lever the stuffing where it's required.

Applying fabric

Simple upholstery pads, such as those in projects 1 and 2 (see pages 34–49) and wings of armchairs, such as those in project 11 (see pages 116–122), will only require one stuffing. Everything else – the arms, back and seat of an armchair for example, will have to be stuffed twice. The first stuffing is covered with a layer of hessian, while the second stuffing is usually covered with calico. A layer of cotton wadding is laid over the calico before the top fabric goes on.

When covering a seat pad with hessian, calico or top fabric, the best way to ensure that the resulting pad is even, is to cut out the covering along the line of the weave and keep the weave straight as you apply it. You can do this by pulling along the line of the weave. If you pull at an angle to the weave, you will stretch and distort the fabric.

Use hessian to cover a first stuffing of fibre. Cut the hessian with enough excess to grip the edge along the line of the weave. Cut a small V in the centre of the front and back edges so that the hessian can be lined up on the chair accurately. Hammer the first four tacks in the middle of the front, back, and each side of the chair. This will help to keep the weave straight as you continue tacking the edges of the covering (see photograph below).

Below Attention to detail is important when doing upholstery. Here you can see that a notch has been cut into the centre of the front edge of the hessian just to help line it up perfectly.

Cotton wadding

Before applying the top fabric you should always have a layer of cotton wadding. This is fleecy cotton that you buy in rolls, usually with a tissue paper backing to hold it together. It's very easy to break apart with your hands and, as a consequence, it sticks to everything including your clothes and the back of the fabric you want to lay over it. This quality makes it perfect for forming the cotton wadding into just the right shape, but terrible for moving fabric around on top of it. The solution is to wrap a very thin layer of synthetic fleece over the top of it first. This adds nothing to the upholstery but allows you to move your fabric into the right position without disturbing the cotton wadding (see steps 1 and 2 right).

1. You can cut cotton wadding from the roll using scissors, but once it's on the area to be covered, breaking it apart with your hands will leave a finer, more even edge. This is an important consideration when working on small, ornate projects.

2. Positioning fabric on a piece such as the Tub chair in project 12 (see pages 124–131) would be almost impossible without a layer of synthetic fleece over the wadding to keep it in place. Lay it over the top, smooth over and tear off any excess – there's no need to tack it in place.

Applying top fabric

The two most important things to think about when applying top fabric, are to make sure the front faces outwards (not so easy with some patterns) and that the pattern is the right way up. The rule for patterns and plain fabrics with a nap to them, for example velvet, is to make sure that it's positioned so that it runs down from top to bottom on the back and arms and continues in the same direction – back to front – on the seat.

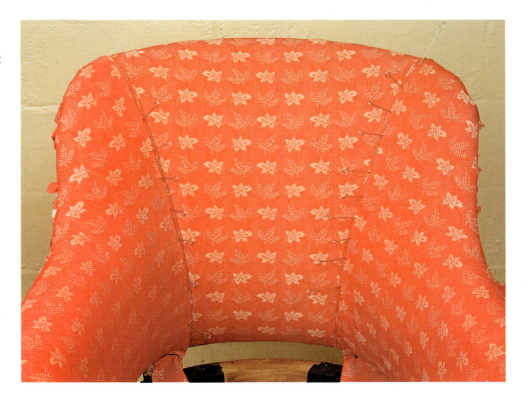

Right Positioning the three pieces of fabric on the inside back and arms of a tub chair is a challenge. The combination of inner and outer curves means that it's impossible to match the pattern perfectly along the seams, but that doesn't matter as long as it all faces the same way and lines up.

Stitching an edge roll

As a general rule any stuffing that is more substantial than a thin pin-cushion pad will need to have the outward-facing edges reinforced to keep them firm and shapely. In traditional upholstery this firming is achieved by sewing rows of stitches in such a way that the stuffing within the pad is pulled tight up to the edge of the covering hessian.

The process is referred to as stitching an edge roll, and consists of one or more rows of blind stitches followed by a final row of open stitches. The stitches are referred to as "blind" because the twine stays within the stuffing. The depth of stuffing will dictate how many rows of blind stitches the edge requires: space each row roughly 12 mm (½ in) apart until you reach a point 2.5 cm (1 in) from the top edge, and then stitch a final row of "open" stitches to form the edge roll (see below).

Before you start, take time to regulate the edge you're about to stitch. Make sure there are no lumps and that the stuffing is even and pulled up to fill the edge. Take a 30 cm (12 in) double-ended needle and thread one end with a length of flax or buttoning twine.

1. Starting at one end of the edge, insert the unthreaded end of the needle just above where the hessian attaches to the frame, or on a seat with a front edge cane, start just above the cane, and at an angle so that the needle emerges from the seat pad a quarter of the way in from the edge.

2. Pull the needle up through the seat pad until just 5 cm (2 in) of the threaded end remains inside the stuffing.

3. Make a sweeping motion, as if drawing a large circle with the free end of the needle.

4. Send the needle back down through the seat pad so that it exits in line with, and 2.5 cm (1 in) along from, the insertion point. Tie a slipknot (see page 18) in one end of the twine and loop it over the exiting point of the needle.

5. Pull the needle out through the slipknot.

6. To complete the stitch remove the needle from the twine and pull the unknotted end tight.

7. Continue repeating steps 1 to 6 to finish the row of edge stitches, but instead of tying a slipknot, as in step 4, simply wind the twine around the needle three times as it exits from the seat pad each time you complete a stitch. Carry on stitching until you reach the end of the row and then tie the twine off.

8. The edge-roll stitches are performed in exactly the same way as the blind stitches except that the needle is inserted so that it exits the same distance in from the edge as it starts below the edge. The needle is then pulled all the way out of the stuffing, so there's no "sweeping" action, and re-inserted into the hessian at the end of the previous stitch.

Through stuffing ties: Using the example of this chaise longue, you can see how stitching the edge roll has transformed the bed from a shapeless pad to a firm-edged, shapely piece of upholstery. You will also notice that there are further rows of stitches running across the top of the bed and the hump. These through stuffing ties are used to flatten and firm up the middle of the stuffing.

Right Sew through-stuffing ties as open stitches in exactly the same manner as edge-roll stitches. Sew them in any shape that is appropriate for the stuffed pad and stitch all the way through from one side of the stuffing to the other, taking care to avoid snagging any springs.

Hand stitching

The majority of stitching is done using a spring needle and flax twine, to stitch the bottoms of springs to webbing, their tops to hessian, or to stitch edge rolls and stuffing ties. A blanket stitch is used to hold the hessian covering tight to the cane on front edge springs and uses the same stitch as whipping (see page 18) but with 2.5 cm (1 in) or so between individual stitches. The two occasions when more formal hand stitching procedures are required are:

1 – when you need to make a join between pieces of top fabric, such as stitching a seam between outside arm and back fabric or to a piped edge, filling a scroll and so on – in which case you use a small curved sewing needle and thread and employ a slip stitch.

2 – when you stitch the hessian, calico or top fabric under the front edge cane on a sprung seat (see project 9, pages 105–107). In which case you use a large, curved sewing needle and strong thread or buttoning twine and employ a locking back stitch.

Slip stitch

1. Make a stitch one side of the seam to be joined.

2. If the seam incorporates piping between the two pieces of fabric, stitch through the piping to the other side of the join.

3. Make a stitch the other side of the seam and continue stitching one side then the other, passing through the piping each time.

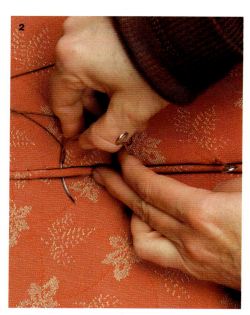

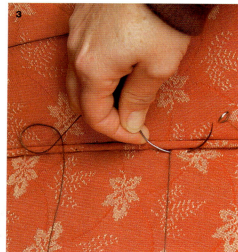

Locking back stitch

Make a stitch by taking the secured end of the twine or thread twice around the needle and then pull the needle through the turns to lock the stitch.

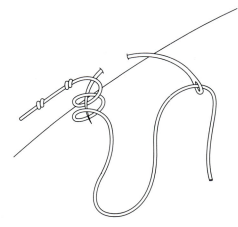

Making single and double piping

Single piping is most often used for cushions, scrolls and finishing edges, while double piping can be used to finish off edges as an alternative to decorative braid or gimp (a form of flat braid). To make piping you need fabric, piping cord and a sewing machine with a zipper foot. For double piping you'll have to buy a double piping foot (pictured below).

1. Lay a piece of fabric out, take one corner, fold it over to the opposite side and cut along the diagonal. Using the diagonal as your guide, cut strips of fabric 5–6 cm (2–2¼ in) wide until you have sufficient strips for the required length of piping.

2. Trim the ends of the strips to the same angle (A). Lay two pieces end to end on the sewing machine, right side up, so that their angles correspond (B). Take one end and turn it over so that the pieces form a right angle, with right sides facing (C). Using an ordinary stitching foot, sew the ends together 12 mm (½ in) from the edge. Join the next strip to the opposite end of the first strip in the same way and continue until you have one strip.

3. Replace your stitching foot with the piping, zipper or double piping foot. Lay the strip of fabric wrong side up, place the piping cord on top and fold the fabric over it. The piping cord can be in the middle if making single piping, but must be towards the outer edge to leave room if making double piping. Drop the piping foot down on to the fabric or, if using a zipper foot, so that the foot rests against the cord, or so that the cord fits into the outer groove if you have a double piping foot. Stitch, folding the fabric over the cord as you go. When you meet a joint in the fabric, flatten it out before you stitch over it.

4. For double piping, lay the single piping wrong side up with new cord running alongside. Fold the already-sewn piping and fabric back over the new cord and lower the double piping foot on top of the two cords. Stitch, folding in the new cord as you go, and trim off the excess fabric when finished.

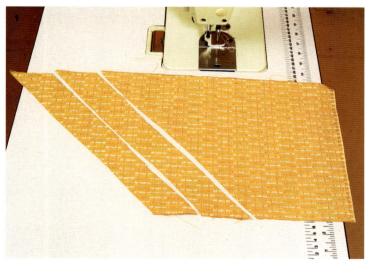

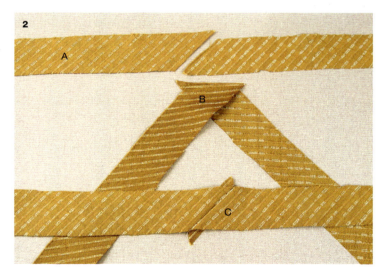

Choosing fabric

Reupholstery is a creative process. The wooden frame of a chair dictates much about the shape and size of the end result, but ultimately it is up to the upholsterer whether to fashion a deep lumbar support, button the back and inside arms, or use piping or decorative cord for the scrolls. Probably the most significant choice to make is that of the top fabric, and it's an important choice.

Most often, this is a matter of personal taste, but a brave choice, rather than a safe one, is likely to produce a more noteworthy result. This generalization is particularly true of the more flamboyant styles of furniture. It's very common to see a Victorian chesterfield's ageless, classical elegance extinguished by green or dusky pink draylon, or a radically shaped Art Deco piece from the Jazz age drowned in a floral slip (loose) cover. If you care enough about a piece of furniture to put in the time and effort to reupholster it, put an equal amount of effort and imagination into choosing the right fabric to finish it in.

Where to buy: Sold by the metre (yard), upholstery fabric can be extremely expensive. An average armchair will require 4–6 m (4⅓–6½ yd) and a two-seater sofa 9–12 m (9¾–13 yd), so even a small amount saved on each length bought can be significant in terms of cost.

Large department stores have accounts with many of the top fabric manufacturers and so offer the widest selection, both in price and style.

Fabric warehouses offer the widest choice of inexpensive fabrics at reduced prices and are certainly worth browsing for bargains.

Small high-street dress-making shops can be one of the best sources of top-quality fabrics at a fraction of the retail price.

Fabric brokers advertise in homes and antiques magazines and will give discounts on the retail price of virtually any fabric as long as you order a minimum of 10 m (11 yd).

What to buy: The fabric you buy has to be suitable for upholstery and not just curtain or dress-making fabric. Sample books will have a key with information on what the fabric is made of, what it is suitable for and the results of various tests it's been subjected to. If you are in any doubt, just ask the retailer. The label or key on any fabric will also state whether it has been treated to make it fire retardant. Just because a fabric is not fire retardant doesn't mean you can't use it, but you should use what's known as a fire-retardant interliner underneath it. This is a fire-retardant calico: it's not expensive and all you do is cover the upholstery with it before laying your fabric over the top.

Leather is sold by the hide. Hides come in different sizes and not all of it is useable, so working out how much you need involves more guesswork than with fabric. If you're going to use leather, don't waste your time shopping around. The best leather costs no more than a good fabric, so find out who makes the best and buy it from them. A reputable leather company will be happy to send out colour samples and give advice on suitability and how much useable leather can be harvested from each hide.

Quality leather won't tear or wear through and any spillages can be wiped off with no ill effect. When your best fabric pieces are looking tired, dirty and in need of a change, the leather armchair you upholstered ten years ago will be growing old gracefully.

Using old fabric: Fabrics from the middle to latter decades of the last century are always interesting to look at as they are invariably either back in style, about to be, or influencing designers producing the next style. Specialist websites are certainly worth a search for quantities of these types of old fabric stock, and internet auction sites can offer up bargains. The use of an interliner can deal with any fire retardant concerns relating to older fabrics and so condition is probably the only consideration in judging whether one is worth using or not.

In most cases replacing tired fabric is the driving force behind a reupholstery project and so reusing what you take off is not really an option.

Measuring up

Before you start stripping an upholstery project it's a good idea to measure it while it still has some shape, so you know how much fabric to buy. Bear in mind, however, that, when finished, your upholstery will be fuller, so don't pull the tape measure too tight against the present shape. If you're starting with just a bare frame, wait until you've got it stuffed and up to the calico stage before measuring.

Here's a diagram of a chair showing the points of measurement you will want to note with their commonly used abbreviations: inside back (ISB); outside back (OSB); inside arm (ISA) and outside arm (OSA).

Take a note pad and write down, in list form from top to bottom: ISB, OSB, ISA, OSA, seat, border, cushion, scrolls, piping, and then measure each area in order. When measuring the ISB, see if you can get its width out of half the width of a fabric roll. (Upholstery fabrics tend to come in rolls 1 m 32 cm to 1 m 37 cm (52 to 54 in) wide, so if the width is 66 cm (26 in) or less, both inside and outside back pieces can come from one complete width.) If this is the case, bracket the two headings together and write the larger of the two measurements next to them. Otherwise, enter the measurement for each. Do the same for the ISA, making sure you tuck your tape well into the crevices in the seat and at the backs and add 7.5 cm (3 in) to the measurement. You should be able to get both inside arms out of one width of fabric, although some chairs have deep seats and require a full width for each. Now measure the OSA, again adding 7.5 cm (3 in). Measure the seat from front to back, tucking your tape well into the seat back and making allowances for a much fuller shape.

Write down the measurement for the seat and note that there will be a large offcut left over from which to find pieces for the scrolls and piping. The seat front will also have to come from a full width. Make allowances in your measurement for turning in at the top and for tacking under the front seat rail.

If your project has a cushion, measure for it, allowing 2.5 cm (1 in) for seams. The top and bottom panels will come from one full width. The cushion border will need two pieces, full width, to the measurement of the depth plus 2.5 cm (1 in) for seams.

Once you have noted all the above measurements, the easiest way to work out how many metres (yards) of fabric you will need is by drawing a cutting plan. This will also show whether there'll be enough from the offcuts to cover the scrolls and make piping. See opposite page for nformation on drawing a cutting plan.

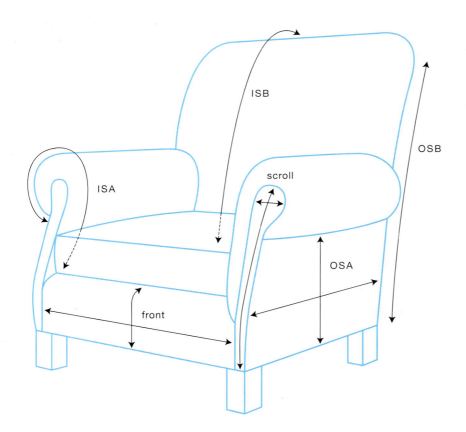

Above You can save fabric and expense by using calico under the portion of a seat covered by the seat cushion.

Drawing a cutting plan

When you draw a cutting plan what you are doing is sketching a representation of a length of fabric as if it had been cut from a roll. You don't need to make it to scale unless you find it easier that way, just get the proportions right and write down the width of the fabric along the top (as shown). The object is to arrange all of the pieces of fabric for each of the elements of the chair – inside back, outside back and so on – on the imaginary roll of fabric and write down their measurements so that you can work out how many metres (yards) of fabric you'll need by totalling up the measurements down the side of the roll. The cutting plan on the right takes its measurements from the list of cutting plan measurements on the far right and shows that the chair will require a minimum total of 5.5 m (6 yd) of material, not allowing for any mistakes. Don't worry about shape; make all the pieces rectangles and arrange them so the biggest go first and try and fit them in in an order that uses the fabric in the most economic way.

Remember that any weave will run along the roll of fabric so plan your pieces so that the direction of the weave runs from top to bottom on backs, arms and wings, and from back to front on seats. Once you have placed all of the main elements of the chair, highlight the waste areas and ensure that they will be sufficient for piping – which will be cut diagonally – and any other pieces for scrolls and such like.

Once you've drawn your cutting plan add 50 cm (20 in) to allow for errors or accidents with scissors, measurements and marker pens. It is well worth developing the habit of sitting down and drawing out a cutting plan for every project you do. They are very simple and are the easiest way to work out with accuracy and confidence the amount of fabric required for any particular project, rather than just guessing 6 m (6½ yd) for a chair and 12 m (13 yd) for a sofa. They also make you focus on what will go in to the upholstery project and how it will all fit together.

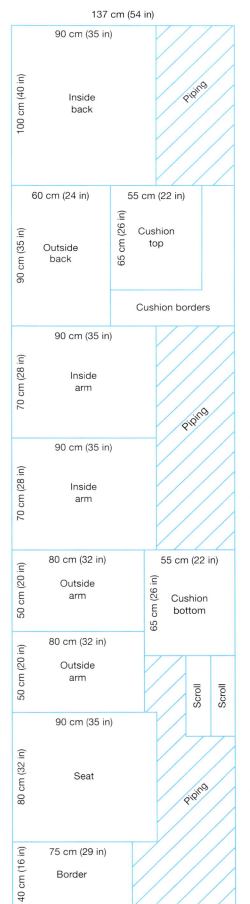

Cutting plan measurements

	cm	in
Inside back	100 x 90	40 x 35
Outside back	90 x 60	35 x 24
Inside arm (1)	70 x 90	28 x 35
Inside arm (2)	70 x 90	28 x 35
Outside arm (1)	50 x 80	20 x 32
Outside arm (2)	50 x 80	20 x 32
Seat	80 x 90	32 x 35
Border	40 x 75	16 x 29
Cushion top	65 x 55	26 x 22
Cushion bottom	65 x 55	26 x 22
Front	10 x 55	4 x 25
Back	12 x 80	5 x 32
Side (1)	50 x 10	20 x 4
Side (2)	50 x 10	20 x 4
Scroll (1)	50 x 15	20 x 6
Scroll (2)	50 x 15	20 x 6
Piping	8m	(8¾yds)

Below A good cutting plan will stop you buying more fabric than you need, and still allow for the small bits you forget.

Making cushion inners

There are many different cushion fillings. Some, like foam, can be inserted straight into a cushion cover, while others – feathers for instance – require you to make an inner cover in which to seal them. If you're going to use feathers – we recommend you use only good-quality duck and down – choose a feather-proof material such as cambric or ticking. Cheap feathers may seem bulky at first, but they'll go flat in no time and won't plump up.

If your cushion is an odd shape, make the inner exactly the same as the outer (see project 7 for details, pages 82–89) but without piping or a zip. All inners can be made the same way as the outer, although there is a very quick and easy way of making an inner for a regular-shaped cushion.

The flat cambric is going to be made into a box shape so you need to measure and cut it out taking into account the depth of the cushion gusset as well as its length and width. Also the inner needs to be slightly larger than the outer so that it fills all the space fully. For example an inner for a 50 cm (20 in) square cushion, 7.5 cm (3 in) deep, would require two pieces 62.5 cm (25 in) square. (50 cm/20 in) + 7.5 cm/3 in plus 2.5 cm/1 in seam allowance and another 2.5 cm/1 in for fullness.)

1. Cut out a piece of cambric and fold it in half or cut two pieces the same size and lay one on top of the other. Stitch all raw edges, making sure you leave a hole big enough to stuff with handfuls of feathers.

2. Take any corner and pull it out so that the seam runs vertically in front of you from top corner to bottom corner.

3. Remembering that the inner needs to be slightly larger than the outer, lay the pulled out corner flat over a ruler, keeping the seam vertical, and mark where the edges are 2.5 cm (1 in) wider than the depth of the cushion outer you're making it for.

4. Lay the corner flat on the sewing machine and stitch from one mark to the other.

5. Repeat this process with the three remaining corners and turn the whole cover inside out. Stuff with feathers and stitch up the hole.

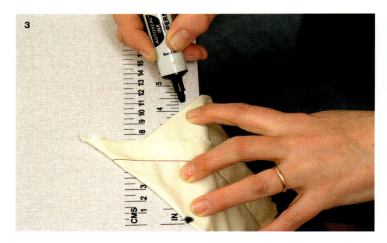

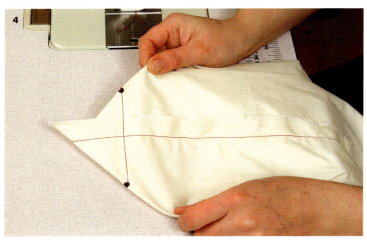

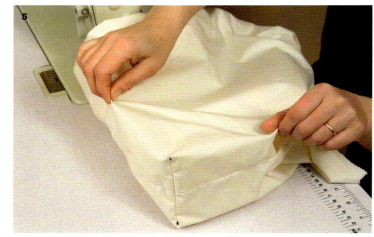

The Van Dyke join

When buttoning an area that requires more than one length of fabric you can join two pieces together invisibly, using the Van Dyke join.

1. In order to differentiate between the two halves, the example here shows two different coloured pieces of velvet with button positions marked in pen.

2. Cut a corresponding zigzag into each piece to be joined. The cut must be made 38 mm (1½ in) in front of the button positions to allow for the seam between the two pieces.

3. Snip into each of the button positions.

4a and b. Turn the two pieces wrong side up and pin together along the line of the zigzag.

5. When sewn together, a button is positioned at each point of fabric and the seam fits invisibly along the folds between the buttons.

BASIC UPHOLSTERY TECHNIQUES

basic skills

1 Drop-in seat 34

2 Pin-cushion seat 42

5 Deep-buttoned stool 66

6 Caning 74

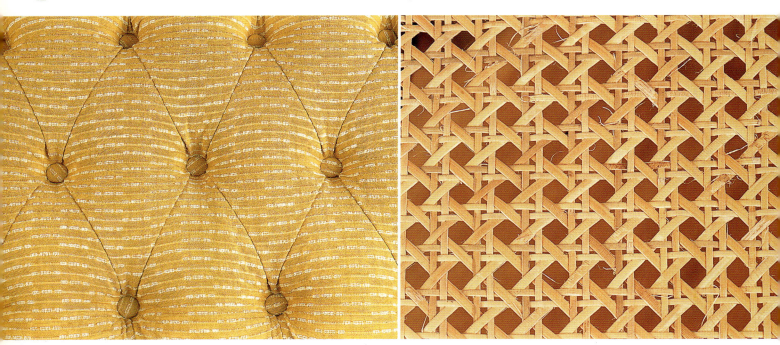

3 Overstuffed seat 50

4 Overstuffed chair with springs 58

7 Box cushion 82

8 Re-covering upholstery 90

1 Drop-in seat

Reupholstering the drop-in seat of a chair is the best way to start learning the skills necessary to move on to more ambitious projects. The procedures are straightforward. Found mainly in dining chairs, but also in some stools, a drop-in seat is a separate, removable seat frame, upholstered and fitted within the seat rails of the chair.

tools

Wooden mallet

Tack lifter

Pincers

Knife

Scissors

Webbing stretcher

Magnetic tack hammer

13 cm (5 in) spring needle

Stuffing regulator

materials

Wood glue

Webbing

13 mm (½ in) and 10 mm (⅜ in) upholstery tacks

Hessian

Flax twine

Vegetable fibre

White and black calico

Wadding

Synthetic fleece

Top fabric

key skills

This small, self-contained project will show you how to achieve the right amount of tension in webbing without over-tightening and help you to gauge the right amount of stuffing to use.

1 Drop-in seat

STRIPPING

1 Remove the seat pad from the chair and strip all existing upholstery from it (see Basic Upholstery Techniques, pages 14–15). Have a good look at the frame to see if it needs any repairs. Don't be overly concerned about tack holes, but if the chair has been upholstered many times you may want to fill the worst of the holes with wood glue and leave to dry before carrying on.

CHECKING FOR FIT

2 It's a good idea to fit the bare frame back into the chair to see how it fits and how big a gap there is around the edges. Your chosen fabric is going to have to fit in whatever gap there is so if it's tight you may have to change your mind about having a thick fabric.

WEBBING

3 Re-web the seat leaving a clear gap between the end of the webbing and the edge of the seat frame (see Basic Upholstery Techniques, page 16). Use 13 mm (½ in) tacks and don't over-tighten webbing on drop-in seats: their frames aren't as strong as normal chair frames and can break.

> **Tip**
>
> As a general rule seats with springs are webbed underneath the frame and seats without springs are webbed on top of the frame. Drop-in seats have a chamfered top edge, so you'll know the difference.

HESSIAN LAYER

4 Cut a piece of hessian large enough to cover the whole of the seat pad with at least 2.5 cm (1 in) overlap all round. Lay it over the webbed frame and tack it down using 10 mm (⅜ in) tacks. There's no need to apply tension, just pull the wrinkles out as you go. Fold the edges of the hessian back on themselves and tack them down. Make sure that you leave at least 13 mm (½ in) of clear wood around the frame so that the chamfered edge is left uncovered.

STUFFING TIES

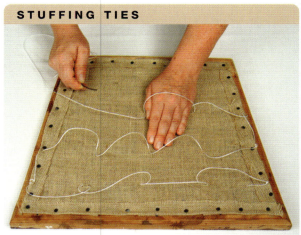

5 Stitch some stuffing ties to the surface of the hessian. Stuffing ties are exaggerated stitches of twine that hold the stuffing in place. Start with a length of flax twine and tie a slipknot to one end (see Basic Upholstery Techniques, page 18). Take a spring needle, stitch through the hessian on the left edge, about 10 cm (4 in) from the top, then pass the twine through the slipknot and pull tight. Use your hand as a guide for the size of the loops and stitch across until you reach the other side, then move down about 10 cm (4 in) and head back across to the edge you started on. Continue stitching the rows of loops until the surface of the hessian is covered.

STUFFING

6 Take a handful of vegetable fibre, discarding any lumps. Tease it into a ball and slip it under one of the stuffing ties. Carry on until the seat frame is covered evenly.

STUFFING

7 How much fibre to use and how tightly to pack it is something you learn by trial and error. When you first start it's natural to underestimate, so bear this in mind. The fibre will pack down and you want a firm pad, so squash it down with your hands to imagine the sort of seat it will make.

1 Drop-in seat

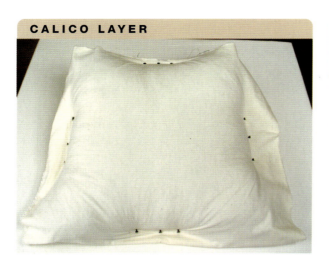

CALICO LAYER

8 When you're happy with the stuffing, cut a piece of calico to fit over it. You will need enough left over to grip and pull, so be generous. Lay the calico over the pad and tack the middle of one side to the edge of the frame. Use 13 mm (½ in) tacks and only knock them in halfway so that they can be removed easily: you're only tacking temporarily at this stage.

CALICO LAYER

9 Using the heel of your hand, smooth and stretch the calico from one side to the other and tack it in place. Continue adding tacks and work your way out from the middle of each side towards the corners.

CALICO LAYER

10 Once all the sides have been tacked, pick the pad up and use a tack lifter to lever out three or four adjacent tacks. Give the free section of calico a final stretch and hold it in place while you replace the tacks. Do this all the way round until the calico is tight and the fibre firmly compressed, then knock all the tacks in fully.

> 📖 **Tip**
>
> Calico layer – fold the piece of calico in half and snip off the corner each end of the fold. The resulting notch will give you the centre points and help you line it up.

REGULATING STUFFING

11 The compacted fibre within the calico will need to be regulated to smooth out any lumps and bumps and to force it into all the corners and edges until the pad feels even and the shape looks regular. To do this take your stuffing regulator, push it into the fibre and simply lever the fibre where you want it to go. Feel for lumps with your free hand and concentrate your effort around the edges.

38 BASIC SKILLS

PADDING

12 Cut out a piece of wadding to fit over the top of the pad and then tease away the edges so that it fits over exactly and the sides are thinned out.

PADDING

13 Wadding breaks up very easily and it is worthwhile covering it with a layer of synthetic fleece to hold it in place and protect it. It isn't essential but it does make working on top of the wadding much easier.

TOP FABRIC

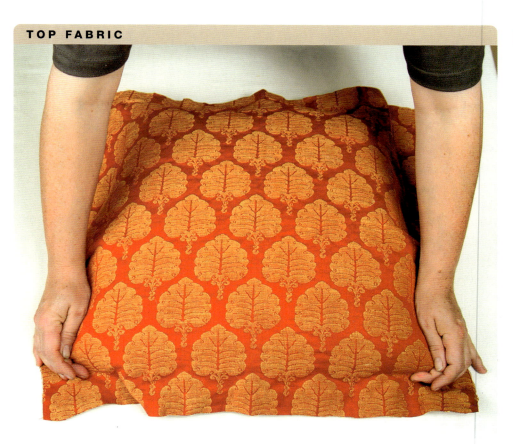

14 Cut out sufficient fabric to fit over the seat pad and fold underneath. Spend time lining up the fabric on the seat to make sure that it's symmetrical, that any prominent feature of the pattern is in the right place and that it's the right way up.

1 Drop-in seat

TOP FABRIC

FINISHING CORNERS

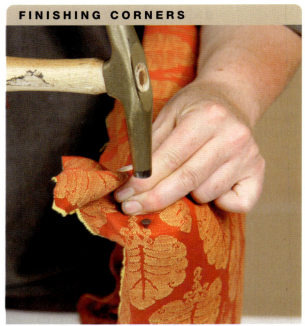

15 Fold the fabric under the edges of the seat pad and temporarily tack it in place with 10 mm (⅜ in) tacks. Start in the middle of the front, then the back and sides, smoothing as you go. Turn it over and check that the fabric is still postitioned correctly before you knock all the tacks home.

16 Finish the corners by pulling the fabric along the front edge so that the fabric on the side and over the angle of the corner is pulled tight. Hammer a 10 mm (⅜ in) tack on the facing edge just back from the corner to hold it in place.

Above Make sure you check to see that your chosen fabric is of a suitable thickness. You don't want to reach this stage only to find that the drop-in seat won't drop in!

FINISHING CORNERS

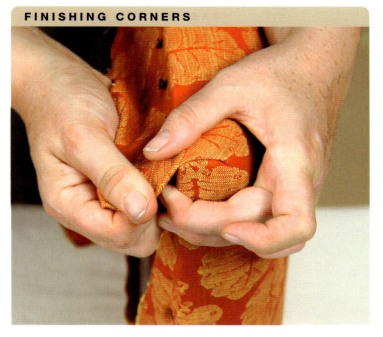

FINISHING CORNERS

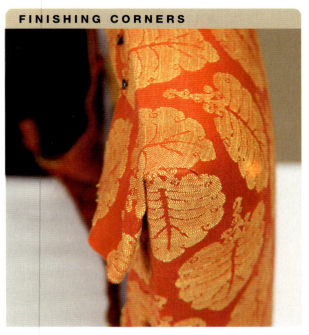

17 Pull the fabric back over so that it covers the tack and form it into a sharp, tight fold on the front facing edge of the corner. Pull the fabric tight under the frame and tack it in place. Turn the pad around and do the other front corner, then the back corners. Ensure that you make all the corner folds so that they lie on the front and rear facing edges of the seat pad and not the sides.

18 If you're good at gift-wrapping you should have a natural feel for how to finish corners on any upholstery project. The secret is to make a few practice folds and as long as you keep the fabric tight and the folds sharp the result will be neat and inconspicuous.

FINISHING OFF

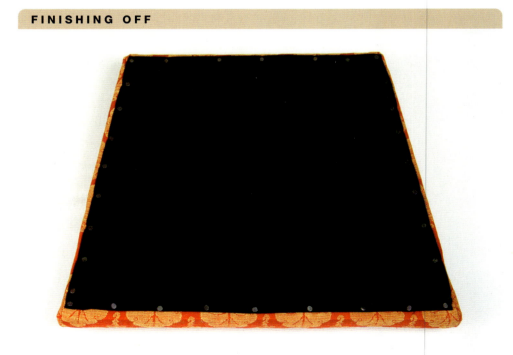

19 The last job, after trimming off any excess fabric, is always to fit a bottom cloth. Cut out a piece of calico: we have used black calico here. Fold the edges under to shape and tack all round.

2 Pin-cushion seat

Pin-cushion upholstery can be found in various places on upholstered furniture, but most commonly as a thin seat pad on a chair. The upholstery is very straightforward, but you are likely to be working in a limited space, so must ensure that the edge of the seat pad is kept free of lumps and bumps from all the materials underneath. The chair in this project is an old office chair, re-covered in leather and edged with upholstery nails, but you can use any fabric.

tools

Wooden mallet

Tack lifter

Pincers

Knife

Scissors

Webbing stretcher

Magnetic tack hammer

13 cm (5 in) spring needle

Stuffing regulator

materials

Wood glue

Webbing

13 mm (½ in) and 10 mm (⅜ in) upholstery tacks

Hessian

Flax or buttoning twine

Vegetable fibre

Calico

Wadding

Synthetic fleece

Top fabric

Dome-headed upholstery nails

key skills

Pin-cushion upholstery teaches you how to work accurately within a confined area. Having limited room to tack webbing, hessian, calico and fabric will force you to work neatly with little waste.

2 Pin-cushion seat

STRIPPING

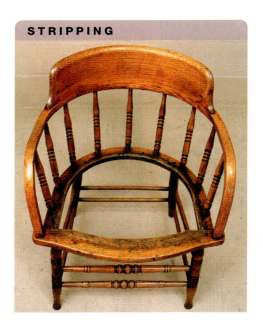

1 Carefully strip all existing upholstery (see Basic Upholstery Techniques, pages 14–15). Pin-cushion seat pads are invariably in the middle of show wood so try not to mark it. If the pad has been replaced a few times in the past you can fill any badly marked areas with a little wood glue and leave it to dry before attaching the webbing.

WEBBING

2 Re-web the top of the seat. Attach the top to bottom pieces first and then weave under and over as you attach the pieces running side to side. If you have to tension your webbing stretcher against show wood place a pad underneath it so that it doesn't cause damage.

WEBBING

3 Leave as much gap as possible between the end of the webbing and where the edge of the seat pad will go. You will have to work in a confined area, but you don't want the ends of the webbing to make lumps along the edges of your finished seat pad.

44 BASIC SKILLS

HESSIAN LAYER

 4 Cut a piece of hessian to cover the area of the seat pad generously and, using 13 mm (½ in) upholstery tacks, tack it in place so that it covers the webbing. There's no need to apply tension, just pull the wrinkles out as you go.

> 📖 **Tip**
>
> When space is tight use only as many tacks as necessary in the early stages so you don't run out of space for tacks and upholstery nails when the time comes to tack on the top fabric.

HESSIAN LAYER

5 Trim around the hessian, leaving 2.5 cm (1 in) excess all round and then fold it back on itself and tack down. As with the webbing, make sure you maintain a gap between the edge of the hessian and where the edge of the seat pad will go.

STUFFING TIES

6 Take a length of flax or buttoning twine and a 13 cm (5 in) spring needle and sew stuffing ties into the hessian (see Basic Upholstery Techniques, page 19). Pin-cushion seat pads aren't as deeply stuffed as other forms of upholstery so make your stuffing ties slightly tighter than usual.

2 Pin-cushion seat

STUFFING

7 Take handfuls of vegetable fibre, discarding any lumps. Tease them into neat balls and tuck one ball under each of the stuffing ties.

STUFFING

8 Continue the process until the whole of the hessian is covered with an even layer of stuffing. Fill in with more fibre if necessary, but remember that this is only a thin upholstered pad, so don't make it too full.

CALICO LAYER

9 Lay a piece of calico over the top of the stuffing, and tack it in place systematically, starting with the middle back, then middle front, and the same with the opposing sides.

CALICO LAYER

10 Apply tension to the calico as you go, so that the stuffing is pulled down to form a tight pad.

📖 Tip

If you are very short of space you can consider using fine-headed tacks or even gimp pins to attach upholstery.

CALICO LAYER	PADDING

11 Trim around the edge of the calico, leaving 2.5 cm (1 in) or so of excess. Fold the excess back on itself and tack down neatly. Upholsterer's shears are very expensive, but well worth the money when you're working in a confined area and need scissors that will cut fine fabric right to their tip.

12 Lay a piece of wadding over the top of the calico and tease the edge away so that it just covers the calico.

PADDING	PADDING

13 Place a layer of synthetic fleece over the top of the wadding to hold it in place over the calico.

14 Trim the fleece so that it covers the calico and wadding without overlap.

2 Pin-cushion seat

TOP FABRIC

15 Spend time aligning your top fabric on the seat pad before you cut it out. Make sure any pattern is the right way round and that any weave runs from back to front.

TOP FABRIC

16 If you're using leather, fold the edges under as you go and tack in place with dome-headed upholstery nails. Any fabric can be finished with upholstery nails, but you can also finish the edges using 10 mm (⅜ in) tacks and then cover with decorative braid or gimp.

48 BASIC SKILLS

TOP FABRIC

17 Put your first nail or tack in the middle back then smooth over to the middle front and place a tack there. Then tack the middle of one side and smooth over and tack the middle of the opposite side.

FINISHING OFF

18 Continue tacking systematically until you've nailed all around the edge of the pad. Using upholstery nails takes a little practice so go slowly and try to keep an even distance between the heads. If using fabric, trim the edge and finish off with double piping, braid or gimp.

Far left Finish corners as neatly as possible and place a nail on the apex.

Left It's a good idea to think about finishing off right at the start of a project – rungs and other obstructions may prevent you using upholstery nails.

Right Don't aim to be too adventurous with your first use of upholstery nails; it's perfectly acceptable to leave gaps between them as long as they are evenly spaced.

3 Overstuffed seat

An overstuffed chair, so called because the seat stuffing goes over the frame, is upholstered like a drop-in seat (see project 1 for detail, pages 34–41), except the seat pad is much deeper. There are no reinforced sides to keep the seat pad in shape, so its edges are packed tight with stuffing, held in with one or more rows of blind stitches, and the top edge is finished with open edge-roll stitches. This is an extremely important upholstery project for the novice upholsterer, since almost all upholstery projects require at least one edge roll to be stitched, and the overstuffed chair provides an uncomplicated introduction as to how, and why, this is done.

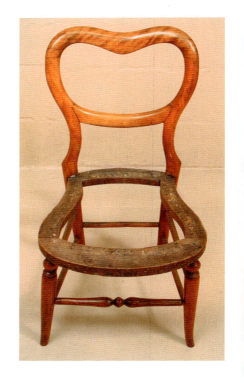

tools

Wooden mallet

Tack lifter

Pincers

Knife

Scissors

Webbing stretcher

Magnetic tack hammer

13 cm (5 in) spring needle

30 cm (12 in) double-ended needle

Stuffing regulator

materials

Webbing

13 mm (½ in) and 10 mm (⅜ in) upholstery tacks

Hessian

Flax or buttoning twine

Vegetable fibre

Black and white calico

Wadding

Synthetic fleece

Top fabric

key skills

This project introduces you to stitching an edge roll. Once you've mastered this the mysteries of traditional upholstery are virtually solved.

watch point

This project introduces you to the double-ended needle. Be careful where it's pointing when you push and pull it, and never leave it sticking out of the seat pad.

3 Overstuffed seat

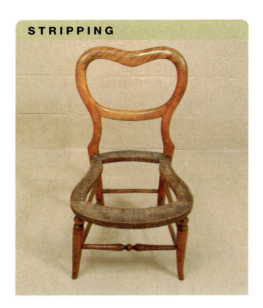

STRIPPING

1 Carefully strip off all existing upholstery (see Basic Upholstery Techniques, pages 14–15).

WEBBING

2 Re-web the top of the seat frame (see Basic Upholstery Techniques, page 16).

FIRST HESSIAN LAYER

3 Attach a layer of hessian over the top of the webbing and stitch stuffing ties across its surface. (See Basic Upholstery Techniques, page 19.)

FIRST STUFFING

4 Take a handful of vegetable fibre, discard any lumps and tease it into a ball. Tuck a ball of fibre under each one of the stuffing ties.

FIRST STUFFING

5 Continue stuffing until the whole seat is covered in a thick even layer. Compact it down with your hands until you judge that there is sufficient stuffing to create a firm pad.

SECOND HESSIAN LAYER

6 Cover the stuffing with hessian, cutting into the corners so that you can pull the fabric down either side of the back supports. Smooth the hessian over and tack front and back and then the sides until the fibre is packed down into a tight pad.

BLIND STITCHING

7 Once the seat pad is formed, take a double-ended needle and, using either flax or buttoning twine, stitch a row of blind stitches all around the pad, about 13 mm (½ in) up from the chair frame. Do this by pushing the needle up into the pad 2.5 cm (1 in) along from the starting point and at an angle so that the top of the needle exits about a third of the way into the seat (see Basic Upholstery Techniques, pages 22–23).

BLIND STITCHING

8 Pull the needle out of the seat until the twine is about to exit and then, using a circular motion, scoop the needle around until it's angled to travel back down towards the row of stitches.

📖 Tip

Buttoning twine is easier to use for edge roll stitching than flax twine. It's strong, smooth and doesn't have irregularities.

3 Overstuffed seat

BLIND STITCHING

9 Push the needle back down so that it exits next to the end of the last stitch. Take the end of the twine and, if it's your first stitch, tie a slipknot to the end of the twine and pass it over the end of the needle. For all subsequent stitches, wind it around the point of the needle three times.

BLIND STITCHING

10 Pull the needle all the way out and pull the stitch tight. Repeat steps 7 – 10 until you have stitched around the entire edge of the pad.

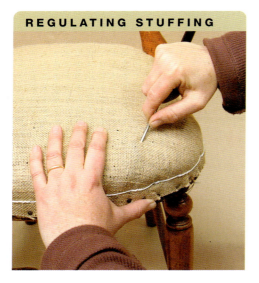

REGULATING STUFFING

11 Use your stuffing regulator to lever stuffing into the edge of the pad after each completed row of blind stitches. Stitch as many rows of blind stitches as are required, spacing them 13 mm (½ in) apart until you reach a point 2.5 cm (1 in) from the top of the seat pad.

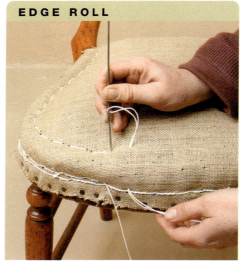

EDGE ROLL

12 The last row of stitches forms the edge roll. Coming from below, angle your needle so that it exits the seat the same distance from the edge as it entered. Pull it all the way out so that the twine exits, move the needle back to the end of the last stitch, push it back down, wind the twine around the end three times, pull it out, and tighten the stitch.

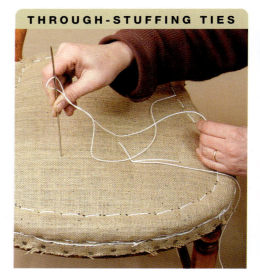

THROUGH-STUFFING TIES

13 Once you have completed the edge roll all the way round the pad you will have formed a firm, shapely edge. To flatten the seat, and to compact the fibre in the middle of the pad, stitch some through-stuffing ties. These are stitched in the same way as the edge roll stitches. Start by going in through the top of the seat.

54 BASIC SKILLS

THROUGH-STUFFING TIES

14 These are open stitches, so pull the needle out of the seat fully before going back in. Tie a slipknot and pass the needle through it for your first stitch. For all subsequent stitches wind the twine around the exiting point of the needle three times, pull the needle through, and pull the stitch tight.

THROUGH-STUFFING TIES

15 Through-stuffing ties compact the fibre and flatten the dome of the seat. They don't need to be as neat as the edge-roll stitches. They do not have to be in rows either, just stitch whatever shape suits the seat.

SECOND STUFFING

16 Carry out a second stuffing in exactly the same way as the first. It needs to be less than half the thickness of the first, so stitch the stuffing ties a little tighter and use much less stuffing.

CALICO LAYER

17 Cover the seat pad in calico this time. Again cut into the corners, pull the calico down either side of the back supports, and smooth over and tack front and back and then each side.

3 Overstuffed seat

CALICO LAYER

18 Temporarily tack the calico in place. Then, easing out a few tacks at a time, give the calico a final pull, hold the tension and replace the tacks.

CALICO LAYER

19 Once the calico has been tensioned down to form a nice, tight pad, hammer all the tacks home fully and trim off the excess calico.

PADDING

20 Cover the seat in a layer of wadding. Use your hands to shape the wadding as this thins the edge. If you use scissors it will leave the edge bulky and may spoil the shape.

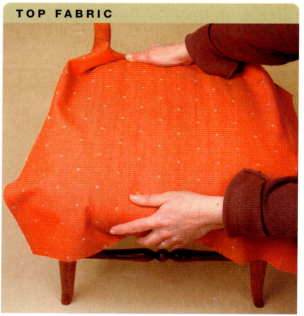

TOP FABRIC

21 Place your top fabric over the seat and make sure the pattern is lined up and that any weave runs from back to front.

TOP FABRIC

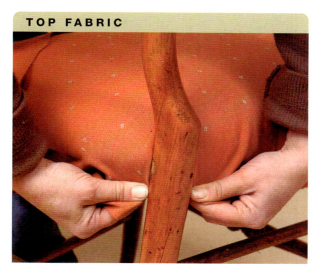

22 Attach the fabric to the seat in the same way as you did the calico, but this time tack it under the seat frame and don't pull it any tighter than is necessary to keep it smooth. Cut into the corners and fold the edges of the fabric where they meet the back supports.

FINISHING OFF

23 Finally, attach a bottom cloth. Cut out a piece of calico: we have used black calico here. Fold the edges under to shape and tack all round.

Above The fabric on this chair is secured under the frame so doesn't need to be finished with decorative trimming.

OVERSTUFFED SEAT 57

4 Overstuffed chair with springs

The chair used in this project is one of a set of Art Deco dining chairs with a sprung overstuffed seat and an upholstered back. With the exception of the seat springs, this project uses the same techniques as project 3 (see pages 50–57 for detail). Springs in seats are usually tied together so that they stay in position and work in unison. It doesn't take long to learn how to tie them (see Basic Upholstery Skills, page 17) and the same principles can be applied to all sprung seats irrespective of shape or size.

tools

Wooden mallet

Tack lifter

Pincers

Knife

Scissors

Webbing stretcher

Magnetic tack hammer

13 cm (5 in) spring needle

30 cm (12 in) double-ended needle

Stuffing regulator

Curved hand-stitching needle

Glue gun

materials

Webbing

16 mm (¾ in), 13 mm (½ in) and 10 mm (⅜ in) upholstery tacks

Springs

Flax twine

Lay cord

Hessian

Vegetable fibre

Calico

Wadding

Synthetic fleece

Top fabric

Cotton thread

Piping cord

key skills

In this project you'll learn to attach and tie seat springs so that they work together.

58 BASIC SKILLS

4 Overstuffed chair with springs

STRIPPING

1 Strip off the existing upholstery (see Basic Upholstery Skills, pages 14–15). Remove the seat webbing with the springs still attached to act as an aid memoir as to how to put them back in.

> 📖 **Tip**
>
> Springs are the same top and bottom. They should be evenly spaced, reasonably close together, but not so close that they interfere with each other.

WEBBING

2 Re-web the seat, tacking the strips to the underside of the chair frame (see Basic Upholstery Skills, page 16).

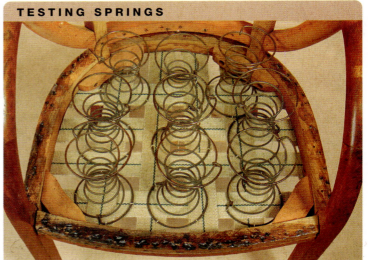

TESTING SPRINGS

3 Test the springs by giving them a good squash between your hands. Replace any that are broken or don't compress evenly. Cut off all the old lay cord and twine and position the springs on top of the new webbing.

ATTACHING SPRINGS	SPRINGING

4 Stitch the springs to the webbing, using flax twine and a spring needle. Four stitches evenly spaced around the base are all that's required.

5 Hammer a 16 mm (¾ in) tack into the seat frame opposite each edge spring, leaving half of the tack protruding. Cut a length of lay cord for each row of springs front to back, and each row side to side. Cut the cord long enough to reach from one side of the chair to the other, allowing for two knots per spring and add 45 cm (17¾ in). Tie one end of the cord to one of the tacks, leaving a 15 cm (6 in) tail.

SPRINGING	SPRINGING

6 Take the lay cord and run it from one side of the chair frame to the other so that it goes over each spring in that row, and tie a clove hitch to the front and back of each top loop as you go. Start and finish by tying the first and last clove hitch to the second loop down (see Basic Upholstery Skills, pages 17–18).

7 When you've tied the last spring in a row, take the cord down to the adjacent tack and back up to the top loop. Apply tension to pull the spring down and then tie it off. Do the same with the first spring in that row. When you've finished, knock both tacks fully home.

4 Overstuffed chair with springs

SPRINGING

8 Tie each row of springs front to back and side to side so that when you're finished the cord forms a grid pattern.

SPRINGING

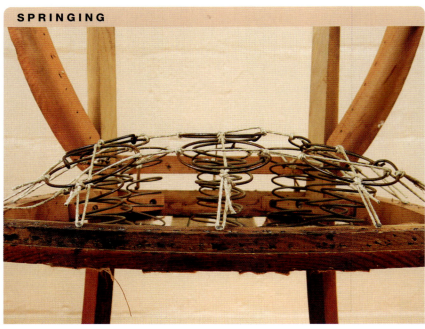

9 If you've tied the springs correctly they will be tensioned down into the rough shape of the seat. They don't need to be overly compressed, their job is to return the seat to its proper shape when the chair is not being sat on.

FIRST HESSIAN LAYER

10 Cover the springs with a layer of hessian. There is no need to tension the hessian, just ensure it lays flat over the springs and isn't baggy.

FIRST HESSIAN LAYER

11 Take your spring needle and flax twine and stitch the tops of the springs to the hessian. Again, four stitches spaced evenly around the top are all that's required. Stitch stuffing ties over the top ready for stuffing.

FIRST STUFFING

12 Carry out a first stuffing of the seat and stitch an edge roll (see Basic Upholstery Techniques, pages 22–23).

COVERING INSIDE BACK

13 The chair shown has an upholstered back, which you can stuff and cover following the steps for a drop-in seat pad (see project 1, pages 34–41 for details).

SECOND STUFFING

14 Carry out a second stuffing on the seat and cover with a layer of calico, then one each of wadding and synthetic fleece to hold the wadding in place while the top fabric is positioned and cut to fit. (See steps 16–21, project 3 pages 55–56 for details).

TOP FABRIC

15 Fit the top fabric around the legs and arms by cutting carefully until you can fold the fabric neatly around the show wood.

4 Overstuffed chair with springs

TOP FABRIC

16 Trim off the excess fabric tight up against any show wood.

PIPING

17 Finish the back of the chair by attaching a length of piping around the back edge, using a curved hand-stitching needle and cotton thread.

Above Make sure your chosen edge trimming covers the tacks holding the fabric on.

COVERING OUTSIDE BACK

18 Tack a layer each of synthetic fleece and calico to the outside back, before hand stitching the top fabric to the piping.

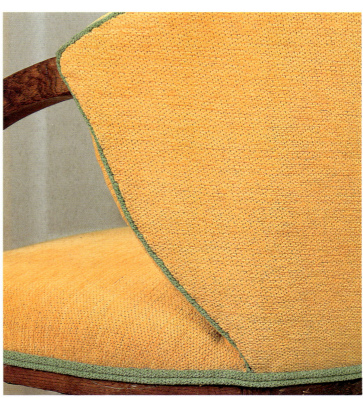

FINISHING OFF

19 Finish the seat with decorative cord, braid or double piping, glued over the top of the tacks securing the seat fabric.

Top and above Contrasting piping was popular in the 1930s – when this chair was made – to accentuate the fashionable "shell" backs of the time.

5 Deep-buttoned stool

A stool is used for this project because it provides a regular, flat shape on which to demonstrate deep buttoning. This example is simply a rectangular frame made out of lengths of pine screwed together, and with cabriole legs attached to each corner. We made the frame and the legs were bought from a craft supplier. You can buy ready-made legs in various styles and shapes so if you fancy designing and making your own stool it couldn't be easier. The procedures for buttoning shown here apply to all other buttoning projects in this book. The technique is not difficult: take care to measure and mark the button positions on the piece and the fabric before you start, and everything will fall into place.

tools

Wooden mallet
Tack lifter
Pincers
Knife
Scissors
Webbing stretcher
Magnetic tack hammer
13 cm (5 in) spring needle
30 cm (12 in) double-ended needle
Stuffing regulator
Metre rule
Upholstery skewers
Marker pen
Tape measure

materials

Webbing
13 mm (½ in) and 10 mm (⅜ in) upholstery tacks
Hessian
Flax and buttoning twine
Vegetable fibre
Calico
Wadding
Synthetic fleece
Top fabric
Covered buttons

 key skills

Deep-buttoning requires accurate measuring out, preparation and attention to detail.

watch point

Call local upholsterers and see if they'll make your buttons. All they need is enough fabric to cover the number of buttons you want. If you do a lot of buttoning work, it might make sense to invest in a button maker, but they are expensive.

5 Deep-buttoned stool

STRIPPING

1 Make a stool, or if you've bought one, strip off all the existing upholstery (see Basic Upholstery Techniques, pages 14–15). The one shown here is simply a rectangular wood frame with cabriole legs attached.

WEBBING

2 Re-web the top of the seat frame (see Basic Upholstery Techniques, page 16). There are no springs in our stool, so the webbing goes on top of the frame.

FIRST HESSIAN LAYER

3 Attach a layer of hessian over the top of the webbing (see step 4, project 1, page 37 for details).

FIRST STUFFING

4 Stitch stuffing ties over the surface of the hessian (see Basic Upholstery Techniques, page 19). Take handfuls of vegetable fibre, discarding any lumps. Tease them into balls and stuff one under each of the stuffing ties. Continue stuffing until the whole seat is covered in a thick, even layer. Compact it down with your hands until you judge that there is sufficient stuffing to make a firm pad.

SECOND HESSIAN LAYER

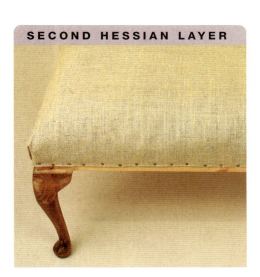

EDGE ROLL

5 Cover the stuffing with hessian, smoothing it over the stuffing and tacking front and back first, then the sides. Fold and tuck corners in neatly.

6 Stitch an edge roll around the pad (see Basic Upholstery Techniques, pages 22–23) The depth of your pad will dictate how many rows of blind stitches are required – here you can see there are two before the "open" edge roll stitches.

SECOND STUFFING

CALICO LAYER

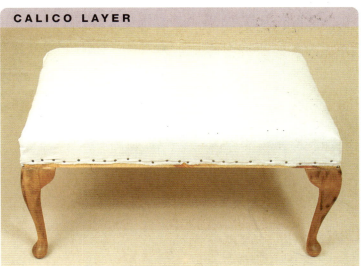

7 Carry out a second stuffing in exactly the same way as the first. It only needs to be half the thickness, so stitch the stuffing ties a little tighter and use half as much stuffing.

8 Cover the seat pad in calico. Temporarily tack the calico in place first. Then ease out a few tacks at a time, give the calico a final pull and replace the tacks. Hammer all the tacks home fully and trim off the excess calico.

5 Deep-buttoned stool

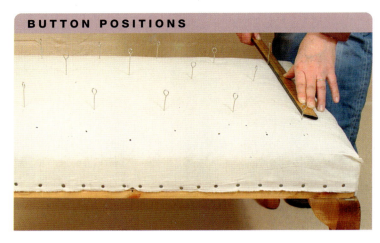

BUTTON POSITIONS

9 Based on the size of the area and the effect you want to achieve, decide how many rows of buttons you will need and how many buttons in each row. With a metre rule and upholstery skewers, rough out where you think the buttons should go. The buttons in any one row should fall halfway between the buttons in the rows above and below.

BUTTON POSITIONS

10 Finalize the button positions, noting down the measurements between the buttons and between the rows, then replace the skewers with crosses, marked on the calico in marker pen.

> 📖 **Tip**
> Use a stitch in coloured thread to mark the button positions on the fabric if you prefer, since using a pen, however carefully, can easily end in disaster!

BUTTON POSITIONS

11 Using a sharp pair of scissors, cut into each of the button positions and excavate down to, but not through, the first bottom layer of hessian.

PADDING

12 Cover the calico with a layer of wadding and a layer of synthetic fleece to hold the wadding in place, then relocate the button positions by pulling the fleece apart with your fingers.

TOP FABRIC

13 Using a flexible tape measure, measure the distance between the centres of adjacent buttonholes. The top fabric will need to travel down into each buttonhole, so add the difference between this measurement and those you noted in step 10 and use the new measurement to mark the button positions on your top fabric.

TOP FABRIC	BUTTONING

14 Position the fabric on the stool and prepare for buttoning. You'll need a 30 cm (12 in) double-ended needle and buttons covered in your chosen fabric. Cut 60 cm (2 ft) lengths of buttoning twine and cut 2.5 cm (1 in) pieces of webbing for each button.

15 Thread a length of buttoning twine through the eye of a button and then both ends through the needle. Start with the middle button position on the bottom row and, with one arm under the fabric to guide the needle, push the needle straight down through the appropriate mark on the fabric, the corresponding button position and through the hessian and webbing covering the base of the stool.

BUTTONING

16 Pull the needle out underneath, taking care not to injure yourself, and leaving the twine and button in place.

Above It is the diamond shapes made by the folds in between deep buttons that give deep-buttoned upholstery its distinctive look.

5 Deep-buttoned stool

BUTTONING

17 Turn the stool over, tie a slipknot (see Basic Upholstery Techniques, page 18) between the two ends of buttoning twine and tighten the knot up on a piece of cut webbing so that the button is pulled down into its position.

Above Deep buttoning isn't as difficult as it at first might seem – a flat surface is the best place to start learning how.

BUTTONING

18 Place all the buttons on the bottom row and then start in the middle of the next row.

BUTTONING

19 With each new button you add, form folds in the fabric between that button and the buttons either side of it. Ensure that all folds face in the same direction.

BUTTONING

20 When all the buttons are in, check to make sure they are all the same depth and the folds are neat.

BUTTONING

21 Make folds from the outside buttons to the edge of the stool and tack the fabric in place under the frame edge.

FINISHING CORNERS

22 Finish the corners as you would for a drop-in seat (see steps 16–18, project 1, pages 40–41 for details) and cover any tacks with double piping, braid or gimp.

FINISHING OFF

23 Tie each of the buttons off with three ordinary knots and trim the ends of the twine. Add a bottom cloth.

6 Caning

Though not strictly upholstery, caning is a skill that every well-rounded upholsterer should have. You will find many chairs with caned seats like the one featured here, or with seagrass or rope seats. Whereas seagrass and rope tend only to be used on seats, however, there are many upholstered sofas and chairs that have cane-filled arms and backs – often referred to as bergère sofas and chairs. If you take the time to learn how to cane, you'll be able to restore these pieces without having to put the work out to a specialist.

tools

Scissors

Hand drill

Hammer

Drill bit the same size as the pegging cane

Bucket of water

Golf tees

materials

No.2 cane for vertical and horizontal strips

No.4 cane for the diagonal strips

No.2 and No.6 cane for beading and pegging

key skills

No upholstery skills required here – just manual dexterity, and the ability to follow a pattern.

6 Caning

STRIPPING

1 Cut away the old cane and remove the pegs from all the cane holes. This usually involves carefully drilling the pegs out, but if you're lucky you may be able to tap out the old pegs using a hammer and an old drill bit the same diameter as the pegs.

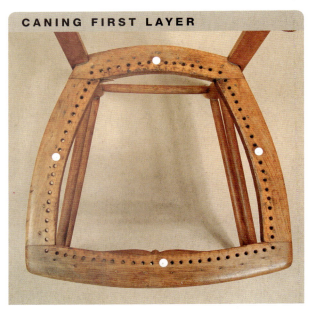

CANING FIRST LAYER

2 Prepare the No.2 cane by soaking it in a bucket of water. Measure and mark the centre hole in each seat rail with golf tees.

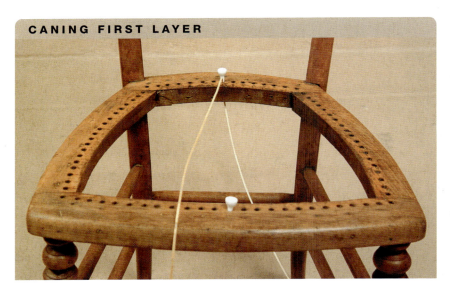

CANING FIRST LAYER

3 Take a long piece of the No.2 cane and, using a golf tee to secure it, peg the cane in the centre back hole, halfway along its length.

> 📖 **Tip**
>
> Allow the cane to soak for a good five minutes and wipe with a cloth before using.

76 BASIC SKILLS

4 With the shiny side of the cane uppermost at all times, pass the length that is above the seat down through the centre hole on the front seat rail, under the frame and back up through the next hole. Pull the cane straight, but not tight, and secure it with another tee.

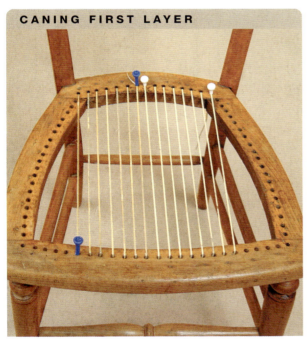

5 Continue caning between the holes, front and back, one side of the centre tee and then the other until you have caned all the holes directly in line with one another.

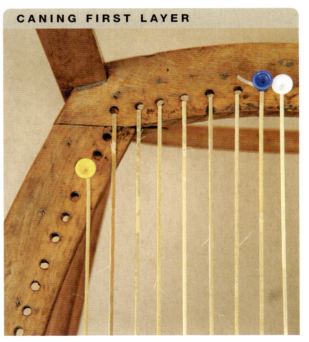

6 If, as with the chair shown here, there are more holes along the front than there are along the back, continue caning from the side holes to the front using new canes secured with tees.

6 Caning

7 Don't use all the side holes, just those that will keep the cane running parallel.

8 Now repeat the process, caning from side to side. Don't weave the cane, just lay it on top of the cane running from front to back.

9 Return to the front-to-back caning and carry out steps 3–7 once more: you can see the process has been started where the blue golf tees are – again, lay the new cane over the top of the rest.

10 Repeat with another set of side-to-side canes, but this time weave them under and over the front-to-back canes.

> **Tip**
>
> Your cane will shrink slightly when dried out so don't tension it too tightly.

CANING SECOND LAYER

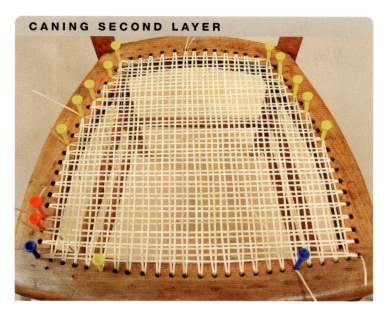

11 With two sets of front-to-back and two sets of side-to-side canes finished, you can now start on the two diagonals.

CANING THIRD LAYER

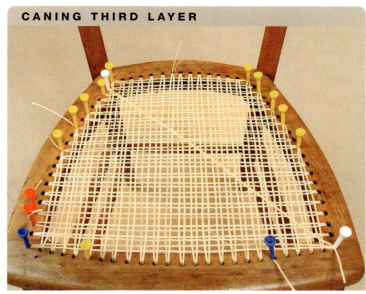

12 Soak some No.4 cane in a bucket of water and, starting at the back corner hole, weave diagonally to the opposite front corner. Weave over the front-to-back canes and under the side-to-side canes as you go.

CANING THIRD LAYER

13 Weave a diagonal from each hole until all the diagonals in one direction have been done.

CANING THIRD LAYER

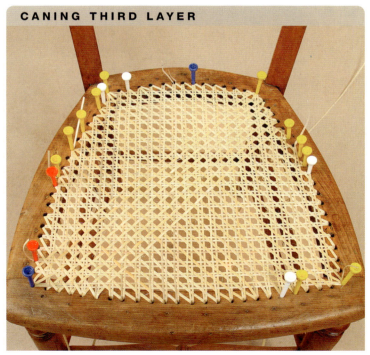

14 Now repeat the process in the opposite direction.

6 Caning

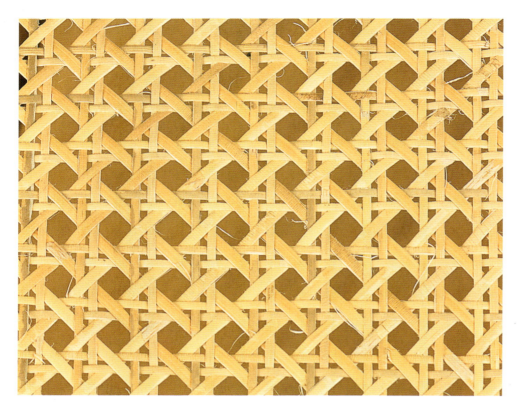

Left If you have a complete section of old cane from your project, keep it handy – if you get stuck you can use it for reference.

Below Caned seats are strong and durable, but are designed to have a seat cushion to help distribute the weight of the sitter.

CANING THIRD LAYER

15 Remove all the tees when you've finished caning and poke all the ends up through the adjacent hole. Every other hole will be plugged so this will ensure that every end is secured.

PLUGGING THE CANE

16 Cut the plugging cane into lengths a little shorter than the depth of the chair frame. Starting with the third hole from each corner, hammer a plug into each alternate hole. When you've finished, cut off the ends of any canes that are poking up.

BEADING

17 Cut a length of beading cane to fit each of the four sides, adding an extra 5 cm (2 in) and trim the ends to fit the holes. Take a long length of No.2 cane and poke one end up into a corner hole. Put the end of the beading cane down into the same hole and peg the two in place. Now loop the No.2 cane up over the beading cane and down into the first corner hole and then each alternate hole pulling tight as you go.

BEADING

18 Continue with the other three lengths of beading cane and finish by hammering a peg into the final corner.

> **Tip**
>
> On some caned furniture the underside of the cane will show, so try and keep everything as neat as possible.

7 Box cushion

This project shows how to make a removable outer box cushion cover to go over a feather-filled inner as part of a low stool. The stool base is square and can be measured accurately, but it is always best to make a paper template of the top surface: this way your seat cushions won't just fit well, they will fit perfectly.

tools

Pen and paper

Scissors

Measuring stick or tape measure

Sewing machine with zipper, piping and sewing feet

Tack hammer

materials

Webbing

Hessian

Top fabric

Piping cord

Sewing thread

Zip

Gimp pins

key skills

Accurate measuring out and your skills with a sewing machine will be exercised here.

7 Box cushion

MEASURING UP

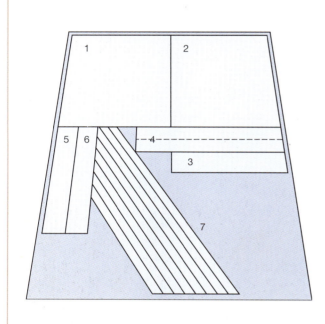

It is important to understand the elements that make up a box cushion and their relative measurements.

Pieces 1 and 2 are the top and bottom pieces of the cover. They should measure 2.5 cm (1 in) bigger all the way around than the size of the finished cushion, to allow 12 mm (½ in) for the seam and 12 mm (½ in) for the fullness of the cushion.

Pieces 3, 4, 5 and 6 make up the cushion gusset. Piece 3 is the front and should measure the same width as piece 1, by the depth you want the cushion to be, plus 2.5 cm (1 in) to allow for a 12 mm (½ in) seam allowance top and bottom. Piece 4 is the zip piece, and will go at the back of the cushion. It should be made long enough to go along the back and 10 cm (4 in) into each side. The depth will be the same as the front piece plus another 25 mm (1 in) to allow for the fabric to fold under 12 mm (½ in) either side of the zip. Pieces 5 and 6 are the side pieces and should measure from the front of the cushion to where the zip piece folds round from the back. They should be the same depth as the front piece.

Pieces labelled 7 are bias strips for piping. Cut as many as you need, 5–7.5 cm (2–3 in) wide.

MAKING UP

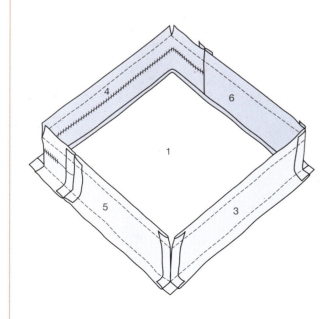

Follow this diagram to see how the top and gusset elements fit together, ready for the bottom to be attached. Note that the cushion is assembled inside out, so remember to open the zip before attaching the bottom, or you won't be able to turn it out the right way. Also note that when the side pieces attach to the front the stitching starts and finishes 12 mm (½ in) in from the top and bottom to allow for the fold of the seam. The zip-to-side join is fully stitched and 12 mm (½ in) cuts made to the top and bottom of the zip piece where it turns the back corners.

MAKING STOOL 	**WEBBING** 

1 If you want to make your own stool, you can buy legs and feet at woodwork shops. Simply make a basic wood frame and attach bun feet to each corner.

2 Web the top of the base and cover the webbing with hessian. Measure the base and draw up a cutting plan.

MEASURING UP 	**CUTTING OUT** 

3 Lay the top fabric right side down on a clean floor and, using your cutting plan, mark out the exact measurements for each of the pieces of the box cushion.

4 Cut out each piece and turn it over so that it is right side up and ready to be stitched together.

> **Tip**
>
> If you intend using a pen to label the backs of the cushion pieces, test it out on an edge of the fabric first – you don't want words showing through after all your hard work.

7 Box cushion

MAKING PIPING

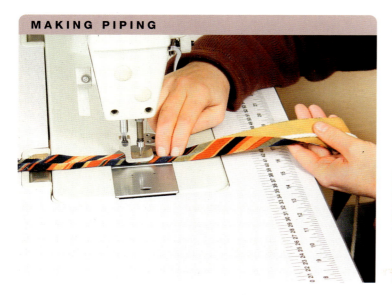

5 First make the piping into one long length (see Basic Upholstery Techniques, page 25).

STITCHING PIPING

6 Leave the piping foot attached to your sewing machine and stitch the piping all around the edge of the top and bottom cushion pieces.

STITCHING PIPING

7 When you come to a corner, snip into the piping flange either side of the angle so that it travels around the corner smoothly.

STITCHING PIPING

8 When you get back to where you started, cut the piping, allowing a 2.5 cm (1 in) overlap, and trim back the piping cord each side of the join.

ATTACHING ZIP

9 Cut the zip piece in half down its length. Change the piping foot for a sewing foot and re-sew the first 5 cm (2 in) of each end.

ATTACHING ZIP

10 Cut a length of zip to fit and lay the zip fabric over the top. Change the sewing foot to a zip foot and stitch the fabric to the zip, folding the edges of the fabric under as you go.

MAKING GUSSET

11 Change the zip foot back to a sewing foot and sew all the gusset pieces together in order, making sure you leave the top and bottom 12 mm (½ in) of the join between front and side pieces unstitched as shown in the photo above.

Above Allowance for "fullness" needs to be made when cutting out the fabric otherwise the finished cushion will lack that comfy look and feel.

7 Box cushion

MAKING GUSSET

MAKING CUSHION COVER

12 This is the gusset sewn together and turned the right way out.

13 Sew the top and gusset together. Some fabrics will make this task harder than others. Velvet, for example, has a strong nap and will tend to move when sewing so that the corners don't meet the joins in the gusset. Take your time and unpick any stitches if it becomes apparent that the fabric has started to creep.

MAKING CUSHION COVER

14 The top and gusset are at the point shown in the diagram above, ready for the bottom piece to be sewn on.

> 📖 **Tip**
>
> It's very easy to get things the wrong way around when making cushion covers, so always double-check each piece before you start sewing.

15 Remember to open the zip before you start sewing the bottom piece to the gusset.

16 Snip across the bulky corners before turning the cover the right way out and stuffing with the cushion inner. (See the Basic Upholstery Techniques, page 30, on how to make a feather-filled inner.)

FINISHING OFF

17 Finish off the stool base by sewing another top piece and gusset together, but this time with four sides and no zip.

FINISHING OFF

18 Tack the cover under the bottom edge of the stool base and attach neatly over the tops of the bun feet with gimp pins.

Far left This project shows just one possible design for a low stool – there are many other styles that you could choose.

BOX CUSHION 89

8 Re-covering upholstery

Re-covering a chair is a very good exercise – particularly if all that needs doing is replacing worn fabric on a chair that is otherwise in very good condition. The way to approach stripping and re-covering is quite simple: start at the bottom, take each step in turn and when the chair has been stripped, repeat the same steps to apply the fabric, only in reverse order.

tools

Mallet

Tack lifters

Scissors

Magnetic tack hammer

Metre rule or straightedge and tape measure

30 cm (12 in) double-ended needle

Upholstery skewers

Sewing needle

materials

Sewing thread

Synthetic fleece

10 mm (⅜ in) upholstery tacks

Top fabric

Buttoning twine

Covered buttons

Webbing

Piping

Tacking strip

Cotton wadding

key skills

In this project you will learn how to carefully remove the top fabric without disturbing the upholstery.

8 Re-covering upholstery

MEASURING UP

1 Take a good look at the chair to make sure it only requires re-covering. Make a note of its measurements so that you can make a cutting plan and calculate the amount of fabric required.

STRIPPING

2 Turn the chair over and remove the bottom cloth. Take care to remove only the tacks or staples holding the fabric. Once the bottom cloth is removed you will gain access to, and can remove, all the tacks fixing the fabric to the underside of the chair.

STRIPPING

3 Remove the outside back, which then gives access to the button ties and the back edge of the outside arms.

STRIPPING

4 Turn the chair over again and remove the outside arm fabric. Once the front and back edges are free, lift the fabric and remove the tacking strip joining it to the underside of the arm. Once all the outside fabric has been removed you will have access to the tacks securing the inside arms, back and seat.

STRIPPING

5 Remove the inside arm and seat fabric and all the tacks holding the back fabric. If the back is buttoned, pull the buttoning cord from behind so that you can get your scissors in under the webbing ties and snip through the cord to release the buttons.

STRIPPING

6 Carefully peel the inside back fabric away to leave the button positions, fold marks and indents as complete as possible.

BUTTON POSITIONS

7 Use the inside back fabric to transfer the button positions to your new fabric. Be careful how you mark the new fabric: the safest method is to make a small stitch using a contrasting thread.

RE-COVERING INSIDE BACK

8 Cover the back of the chair with a layer of synthetic fleece, tucked in to hold it in place under the fabric.

BUTTONING

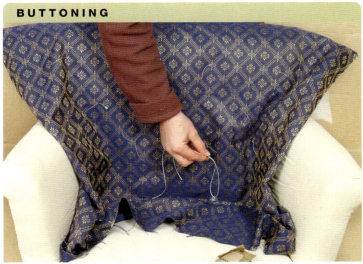

9 Place the new inside back fabric over the back of the chair and, starting with the bottom row, work your way up a row at a time to replace the buttons (see steps 15–16, project 5, pages 71–72 for details).

> **Tip**
>
> Find a modern chair with deep buttons to use in this project – using the old buttoned fabric as a template will allow you to practise and gain confidence in your buttoning skills.

8 Re-covering upholstery

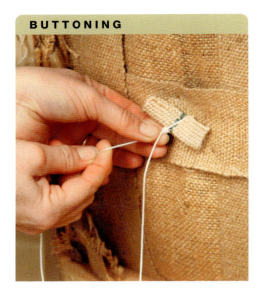

BUTTONING

10 At the back of the chair, tie a slipknot between the two ends of the buttoning twine and pull up tight against a piece of webbing to hold the button in place.

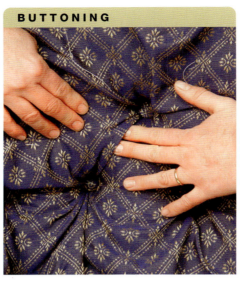

BUTTONING

11 Fold the fabric between the buttons in one row before moving on to the next.

BUTTONING

12 When all the buttons are in place, lift the bottom edge of the fabric and make cuts in the synthetic fleece, straight down from the buttons in the bottom row.

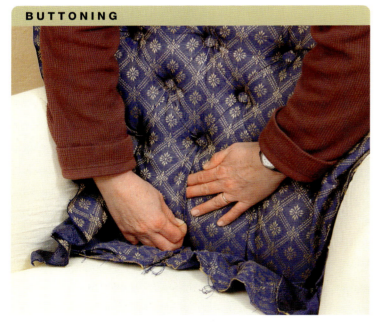

BUTTONING

13 Replace the top fabric and make folds that correspond to the cuts you've just made. Tuck the fabric down behind the seat and secure it, with folds intact, under the back rail. Finish the top and sides of the back in the same way.

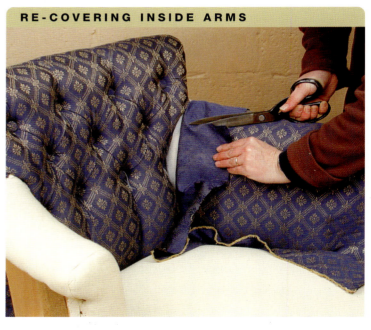

RE-COVERING INSIDE ARMS

14 Once the inside back fabric is in place, re-cover the inside arms, adding a layer of synthetic fleece first and making cuts where appropriate, to allow the fabric to tuck into the chair frame.

94 BASIC SKILLS

RE-COVERING SEAT

15 Replace the seat fabric next, again adding a layer of synthetic fleece, and cut into the back and sides of the fabric so that it tucks around the chair frame.

RE-COVERING SEAT

16 Secure the front edge of the seat fabric with upholstery skewers and hand stitch in place, using locking back stitch (see Basic Upholstery Techniques, page 24, for details).

RE-COVERING SEAT

17 Make up a piped, or trimmed, valance for the front edge of the seat, ensuring it's wide enough to be secured below the outside arm fabric. Hand stitch the top of the valance to the front edge of the seat fabric and tack it under the front edge of the seat and around the sides.

RE-COVERING OUTSIDE ARMS

18 The outside arms are next. Fold the top edge of the fabric under and secure in place under the arm roll with skewers.

> **📖 Tip**
>
> If there's not enough fabric to be pulled under the frame where the seat meets the front of the arm, stitch a couple of lengths of buttoning twine to the fabric so you can pull down and attach it to the frame.

8 Re-covering upholstery

RE-COVERING OUTSIDE ARMS

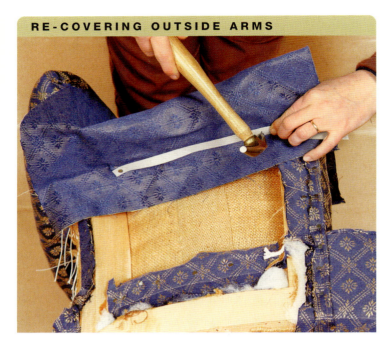

19 Lift the outside arm fabric up over the arm and tack the top edge to the underside of the arm roll, using a length of tacking strip to give a straight edge to the join.

RE-COVERING OUTSIDE ARMS

20 Pull the outside arm fabric back down, tack it under the chair frame and then to the front and back edges. The front edge on this chair doesn't have a scroll so is finished with a length of piping hand stitched in place.

RE-COVERING OUTSIDE BACK

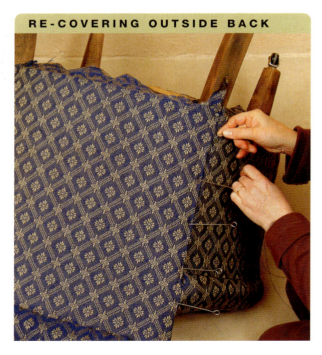

21 Once the outside arms are finished, replace the outside back in exactly the same way and hand stitch where it meets the outside arms.

SCROLLS

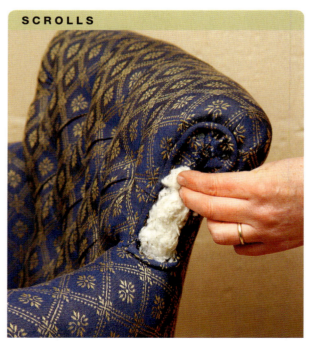

22 If the chair has any scrolls, attach either piping or other trimming around their edges and pad the inside with a little wadding.

SCROLLS

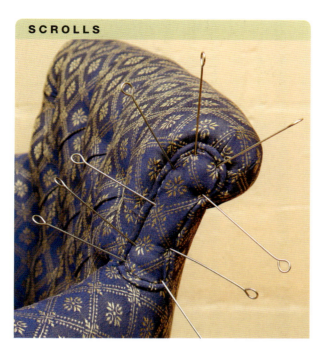

23 Carefully fit a piece of fabric within the trimming, hold it in place with skewers and hand stitch all around the edge. See Basic Upholstery Techniques, page 24, for details.

FINISHING OFF

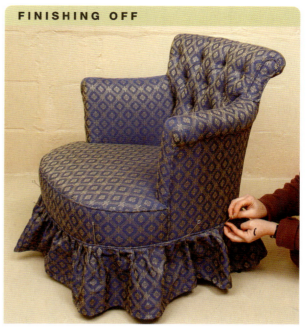

24 Make and reattach any skirt (see caption below right) and replace the bottom cloth.

Above When filling in scrolls keep the nap and pattern of the fabric running from top to bottom.

Above Often you'll have to make up a new skirt by carefully removing and copying the dimensions of the old one.

RE-COVERING UPHOLSTERY 97

applying basic

9   Art Deco armchair 100

10   Classic armchair 108

13   Chaise longue 132

14   Drop-arm sofa 140

skills

11 Wing chair 116

12 Tub chair 124

15 Buttoned leather chesterfield 148

Art Deco armchair

A project like this is invaluable for helping you to visualize the order in which to do things. The aim is that you will be able to look at a piece you haven't upholstered before and work out how to arrive at the end result without getting into difficulty. This chair also introduces front-edge seat springs. On most substantial chairs and sofas the front edge of the seat has a separate row of springs. They are whipped to a cane along their front edge and tied down so that they are all the same height. Once covered in hessian, a trench is made between the two sets of springs, which is subsequently stuffed with fibre. The combination of front-edge springs, cane and fibre stuffing give an extremely firm front edge to the finished chair or sofa.

tools

Wooden mallet

Tack lifter

Pincers

Knife

Scissors

Webbing stretcher

Magnetic tack hammer

13 cm (5 in) spring needle

30 cm (12 in) double-ended needle

Stuffing regulator

Ruler

Curved hand-stitching needle

Upholstery skewers or pins

materials

Webbing

16 mm (¾ in), 13 mm (½ in) and 10 mm (⅜ in) upholstery tacks

Springs

Flax and buttoning twine

Lay cord

Cane

Hessian

Vegetable fibre

Calico

Wadding

Synthetic fleece

Piping cord

Top fabric

Cotton thread

key skills

This project involves advanced seat springing and working out the order in which to complete the combined elements of the back seat and arms.

9 Art Deco armchair

STRIPPING

1 Strip off all existing upholstery (see Basic Upholstery Techniques, pages 14–15). Where possible, leave the springs attached to the webbing so that you can see their original configuration when the time comes to put them back.

WEBBING

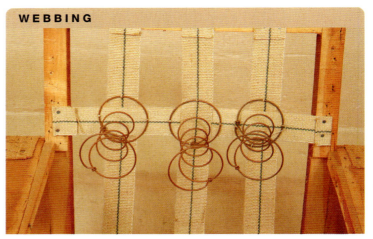

2 Re-web the seat and back (see Basic Upholstery Techniques, page 16), and stitch in the back springs.

FIRST HESSIAN LAYER

3 Cover the back springs with hessian so that they are squashed down by about a quarter of their height and stitch the tops of the springs in position. Attach the hessian top and bottom, but only above the arms at the sides. Leave the sides below the arms open so that arm and subsequent back coverings can be pulled through.

FIRST STUFFING

4 Stuff the back, cover with another layer of hessian and regulate out any unevenness in the stuffing.

CHECKING SEAT SPRINGS

5 Check the original seat springs, replace any that are broken or don't compress evenly and cut off all the old lay cord and twine. Stitch the seat springs back into the seat and tie with new lay cord (see Basic Upholstery Techniques, page 17).

CHECKING SEAT SPRINGS

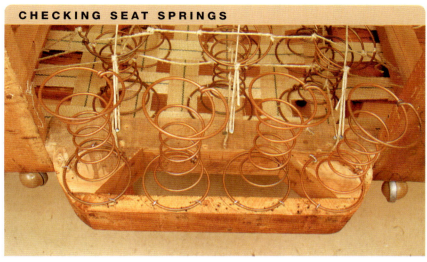

6 Check the original front-edge seat springs and replace any broken ones. Reattach them to the front of the seat frame using either netting staples or webbing secured over their bases.

ATTACHING CANE

7 Whip the front-edge cane to the edge springs (see Basic Upholstery Techniques, page 18). If the old cane is straight and in one piece reuse it, otherwise replace with a new piece or, if no cane is available, use a straightened spring wire.

FRONT-EDGE SPRINGS

8 Tie down each of the front-edge springs so that they are compressed to the desired height and the cane is held straight and level. Use lay cord and tie one end to the back of the bottom turn of the spring and take it up to the back of the top turn and tie the back of the spring down to the desired height. Then take the cord to the front of the spring, over the cane and down to a tack on the front of the frame. Use a ruler to get the springs the same height and make any adjustments to the knots before hammering the securing tack home.

9 Art Deco armchair

FRONT-EDGE SPRINGS

9 Cut a length of webbing in half lengthwise. Tack one end of the webbing to the front of the seat frame slightly to one side of a front edge spring. Take the webbing up and over the front edge of the middle turn of the spring and then tack it the same distance the other side of the spring so that it forms an inverted V-shape. Do this with each of the front-edge springs. This will stop the front-edge springs being pushed back into the seat.

MAKING THE TRENCH

10 Cover the seat and front-edge springs with a piece of hessian. Tack the hessian in position over the seat springs, but don't tack it over the front-edge springs yet. Use your hand to make a trench in the hessian between the seat and front-edge springs, and secure a length of lay cord tight across it using a tack on each side of the front seat rails.

MAKING THE TRENCH

11 Peel back the portion of the hessian that will cover the front-edge springs. Using a spring needle and buttoning twine, stitch lengths of twine through the hessian over the lay cord. Pull the cord tight so that it holds the lay cord down into the trench and secure it to a tack positioned wherever is convenient on the front edge of the frame. Do this at intervals along the length of the lay cord, making sure not to snag the front-edge springs.

ATTACHING HESSIAN

12 Pull the front of the hessian back over the front-edge springs and tack it along the front edge of the frame. Take some flax twine and blanket-stitch all along the caned front edge (see Basic Upholstery Techniques, page 24). Stitch the tops of the seat and front-edge springs to the hessian. Carry out a first stuffing of the seat, packing the fibre firmly between the seat and edge springs.

 Tip

When stuffing the seat make sure the stuffing is wide and deep enough to fill the gaps between the bottom of the inside back and inside arms.

SECOND STUFFING

13 Tack the back and sides of the hessian covering the seat stuffing and pull the front tight over the caned edge. Secure with skewers under the cane. Stitch in place under the cane with flax twine and then stitch an edge roll along the front edge. Carry out a second stuffing of the inside back and seat, finishing each surface with a layer of calico. Stitch the front edge under the edge roll with flax twine. If the chair has a seat cushion stretch a piece of webbing tightly over the seat a third of the way from the front edge and secure either side of the frame. This will create a depression in the seat to encourage the cushion to sit down into the seat and not slide off the front.

Above Flat-topped arms were all the rage when this chair was made in around 1933.

PADDING ARMS

14 Cover the tops of the arms with a layer of wadding and synthetic fleece to hold the wadding in place.

COVERING ARMS

15 Now cover the tops of the arms and tack the fabric in place along the inner and outer edges of the arm frames.

COVERING ARMS

16 Make some piping (see Basic Upholstery Techniques, page 25) and tack it all along the inside and outside edges of both arms. Fill the insides of the arms with a layer of hessian.

9 Art Deco armchair

COVERING ARMS

17 Cover the hessian with synthetic fleece. Tack the bottom edge of the inner arm fabric to the lower arm rail and hand stitch the top edge to the piping using a curved hand-stitching needle and cotton thread. Hold the fabric in position using upholstery skewers or pins and stitch the fabric to the piping and the piping to the top arm fabric at the same time.

FINISHING SEAT

18 Cover the seat with a layer of wadding and synthetic fleece and then cover with the top fabric. Tack the back and sides in place and skewer the front edge under the cane before hand stitching with strong twine.

FINISHING INSIDE BACK

19 Cover the inside back with a layer of wadding and synthetic fleece and then cover with the top fabric. Make sure your fabric is positioned correctly before making any cuts to the sides where it goes around the arm frames.

FINISHING FRONT EDGE

20 Make up a piece of fabric with piping sewn along the top edge, then pin and hand stitch it in place along the front edge of the seat fabric.

FINISHING FRONT EDGE

21 Lift up the front edge fabric, stitch some stuffing ties all the way along its length and apply a thin layer of stuffing.

FINISHING FRONT EDGE

22 Pull the front-edge fabric over the stuffing and tack it under the front of the seat frame. Pull the edges through between the seat and arms and secure inside the arms.

Above A meticulous cutting plan will ensure that patterns on backs and seat cushions line up nicely.

FINISHING OFF

23 Finish the outside arms in the same way as the inside arms and finish off by hand stitching the outside arm fabric to the piping around the outside arm edges. Tack piping around the edges of the back and backs of the arms and apply the outside back fabric in the same way you did the outside arms. Cover the underside with a bottom cloth and make a box cushion for the seat (see steps 2–16, project 7, pages 84–89 for details).

10 Classic armchair

This classic-shaped late-Victorian armchair follows on from the previous project in that it has the same front edge and seat spring combination. The arms on this chair, however, are also sprung, are stuffed and have scrolls on their fronts. The initial stages of stuffing the arm require the fronts to have a stitched edge roll. Chairs like this were very common throughout the late 19th and early 20th centuries and form the classic shape for chairs and sofas made today. Variations often come with scrolls on the sides of the back above the arms.

tools

Wooden mallet

Tack lifter

Pincers

Knife

Scissors

Webbing stretcher

Magnetic tack hammer

13 cm (5 in) spring needle

30 cm (12 in) double-ended needle

Stuffing regulator

Curved hand-stitching needle

materials

Webbing

16 mm (⅝ in), 13 mm (½ in) and 10 mm (⅜ in) upholstery tacks

Springs

Flax twine

Lay cord

Hessian

Vegetable fibre

Calico

Wadding

Synthetic fleece

Top fabric

Cotton thread

Decorative cord

Braid

key skills

Stitching an edge roll to scrolls and covering sprung arms are the skills that you will learn in this project.

10 Classic armchair

STRIPPING

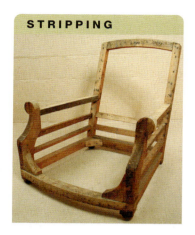

1 Strip off all existing upholstery (see Basic Upholstery Techniques, pages 14–15). Where possible, leave any springs attached to the webbing so that you can see their original configuration when the time comes to put them back.

WEBBING

2 Re-web the back and replace the back springs. The back doesn't take as much weight as the seat so you don't need to use a stretcher to get the webbing really tight. You can use one if it's easier, but you should be able to pull it tight enough by hand.

INSIDE BACK

3 Cover the back springs with hessian and stitch the tops in place. A chair like this will be more comfortable with a little more stuffing in the lumbar area. Rather than trying to stuff the back unevenly, apply a preliminary stuffing to the lower half of the back at this stage, and cover it over with hessian.

ARM SPRINGS

4 Note the position of arm springs when stripping off and secure them back in place by tacking webbing over their bases. Tack another piece of webbing to the back of the arm, pull over the tops of the springs so that they are squashed down and tack it to the top of the scroll. Make sure that the springs are sitting vertically and stitch their tops to the webbing using a spring needle and flax twine.

INSIDE ARM

5 Tack a strip of webbing between the top and bottom rungs in the middle of the inside arm to add a little support, and another 5 cm (2 in) in from the back. The second piece of webbing creates a back edge to the inside arm and a gap between the arm and back through which to tuck the hessian, calico and top fabric. Cover the inside arm and springs with hessian.

STUFFING AND COVERING ARMS

6 Stuff the back and arms and cover with another layer of hessian. Cover the arm stuffing by tacking the bottom edge of the hessian to the bottom inside rung of the arm first and then use the palm of your free hand to smooth it up, over the arm roll and under the top rung. Tack it in place so that it creates an even roll of stuffing over the top of the arm. Tuck the back edge of the hessian through the gap between the webbing and the back, pull it back towards the front of the chair and use skewers to hold it there for the time being.

ARM SCROLL

7 Position yourself in front of the arm scroll and smooth the hessian from back to front and then fold the front edge under where it meets the edge of the scroll. Use your free hand to hold the folded edge in place and tack the hessian to the edge of the scroll. Space the tacks 5 cm (2 in) apart to hold the shape first, and then go back and tack in between them.

ARM SCROLL

8 Take your time tacking the hessian around the scroll and aim to finish with a neat, closely tacked edge.

EDGE ROLL

9 Regulate the stuffing so that it's even and smooth, then stitch an edge roll to the scrolls and through-stuffing ties to the back and arms (see Basic Upholstery Techniques, pages 22–23).

> **Tip**
>
> If you can feel springs through the stuffing then you need to insert more stuffing.

CLASSIC ARMCHAIR 111

10 Classic armchair

SEAT SPRINGS

10 Re-web the seat, and spring (see steps 5–9, project 9, pages 103–104 for details). Note that the cane along the front-edge springs is attached to the fronts of the arms with two pieces of webbing so that it forms the same shape as the bottom edge of the seat frame.

> **Tip**
>
> Where canes aren't attached to the fronts of the arms, tuck all material layers between the arm and seat front.

STUFFING SEAT

11 Cover the seat springs with hessian (see steps 10–12, project 9, page 104 for details) and carry out first and second stuffings of the seat and second stuffings of the back and arms, finishing with a layer of calico on each surface. Apply a layer of wadding to the inside back, cover with synthetic fleece to hold it in place, and then cover with your top fabric. Make cuts to the back fabric where necessary so that it fits around the arm frames, make folds along the top corners of the back, and tuck excess fabric through the back edge of the arms and tack in place.

Above All corners are different, so experiment with folds until you achieve a solution that is as neat and as in keeping with the shape of the chair as possible, before securing the fabric.

COVERING INSIDE ARMS

12 Cover the inside arms next. Apply a layer of wadding and fleece first, then the top fabric, repeating steps 6, 7 and 8. Tack the back edge of the arm fabric to the back frame and then, where, in step 6, you pulled the back edge hessian and calico back on itself and skewered it out of the way, remove the skewers and attach it to the back frame on top of the fabric.

COVERING SEAT

13 Next cover the seat with wadding, fleece and then the top fabric. Stitch the front edge of the seat fabric under the front lip using strong twine and tack the back and sides to the seat rails.

COVERING SEAT

14 Stitch a piece of fabric to the front panel of the seat using a curved hand-stitching needle and cotton thread.

COVERING SEAT

15 Lift the front edge fabric, stitch some stuffing ties and stuff the front panel, and then pull the fabric back over the front and tack under the front seat frame.

FINISHING FRONT

16 To hide the join between the seat and front edge fabric stitch a length of decorative cord along it.

COVERING OUTSIDE ARM

17 Using tacking strip, secure the outside arm fabric to the under edge of the arm.

COVERING OUTSIDE ARM

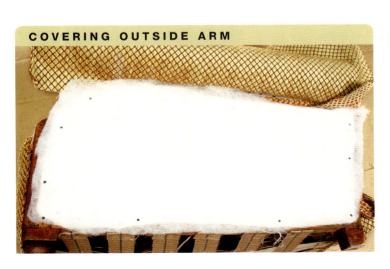

18 Pull back the top fabric while you fill the area under the outside arm with a piece of calico and cover it with synthetic fleece.

📖 Tip

If you are using piping instead of decorative cord, sew the front piece fabric and piping together first before attaching them to the front panel of the seat.

10 Classic armchair

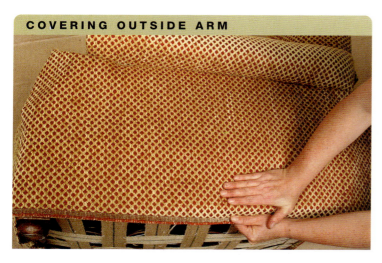

COVERING OUTSIDE ARM

19 Pull the top fabric over the calico and fleece and tack it in place under the seat frame first, and then the back frame and front edge of the scrolls. Once the outside arms have been covered, the back fabric is stitched in place along the top and sides and tacked under the back seat frame.

FINISHING ARMS

20 Finish the scrolls by padding the area to be filled with pieces of wadding.

FINISHING ARMS

21 Cut out a piece of fabric to fill the scrolls, fold the edges under into the shape of the scrolls and skewer in place before stitching, using a curved hand-stitching needle and cotton thread.

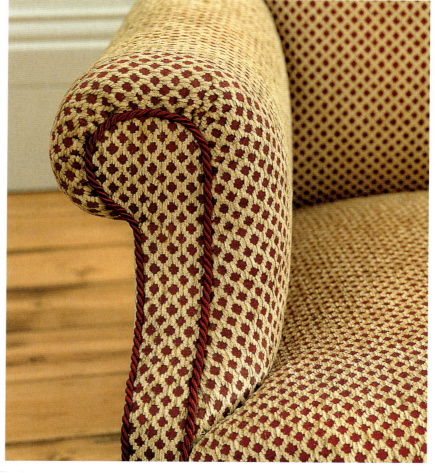

FINISHING ARMS

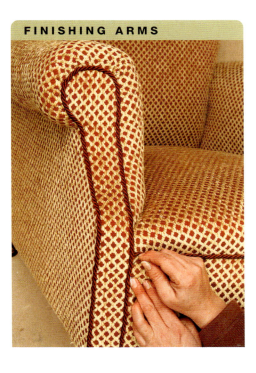

22 Hand stitch decorative cord to frame the scrolls and to hide the join between the arm and scroll fabric.

FINISHING OFF

23 Finish off the bottom edge of the chair with braid the same colour as the decorative cord either by gluing or tacking in place with coloured gimp pins. Finally, apply a bottom cloth.

Left Decorative cord is a good alternative to piping, especially if you want to highlight features such as scrolls.

Right There's nothing wrong with combining several trimmings such as braid and cord, as long as they are an exact colour match.

CLASSIC ARMCHAIR

11 Wing chair

A wing chair is extremely satisfying to upholster. It is not as complicated a project as it might appear and, once finished, makes an impressive showcase for your upholstery skills. Wing chairs come in various shapes, sizes and styles but, in essence, they are simply armchairs with tall backs and wings; and that's how you approach upholstering them. This project will concentrate on the detail of how to upholster the wings. Refer to project 10, for upholstering the seat, arms and back (see pages 110–115) and Project 7 for making up the seat cushion (see pages 82–89).

tools

Wooden mallet
Tack lifter
Pincers
Knife
Scissors
Webbing stretcher
Magnetic tack hammer
13 cm (5 in) spring needle
30 cm (12 in) double-ended needle
Stuffing regulator
Upholstery skewers
Curved hand-stitching needle

materials

Webbing
13 mm (½ in) and 10 mm (⅜ in) upholstery tacks
Springs
Flax twine
Lay cord
Hessian
Vegetable fibre
Calico
Wadding
Synthetic fleece
Top fabric
Cotton thread
Piping cord

key skills

This project introduces you to upholstering wings and making a well-fitting seat cushion.

11 Wing chair

STRIPPING

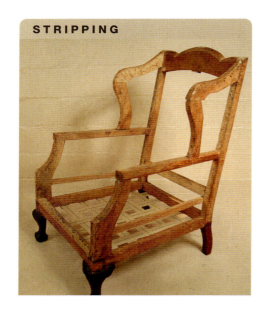

1 Strip off all existing upholstery (see Basic Upholstery Techniques, pages 14–15). Note any interesting details so you can refer to them later when you come to reupholster the piece.

WEBBING AND SPRINGING

2 Re-web the seat, back and arms (see Basic Upholstery Techniques, page 16). Reinstall the seat, back and arm springs if it has them (our chair had only seat springs). Cover the seat, back and arms in hessian and stitch the tops of the springs to it.

FIRST HESSIAN LAYER

3 Attach a strip of webbing to the frame of the wing 5 cm (2 in) in from where it attaches to the back, then cover the inside of the wing with hessian. Tack the hessian to the inside of the wing frame and the top of the arm, and stitch it to the webbing to hold its back edge in place: don't attach it to the back frame. (You can see the webbing and stitches in step 6.)

> **Tip**
>
> Before stuffing the inside arms, sit in the seat so that you can judge how much seat space is required.

118 APPLYING BASIC SKILLS

FIRST STUFFING

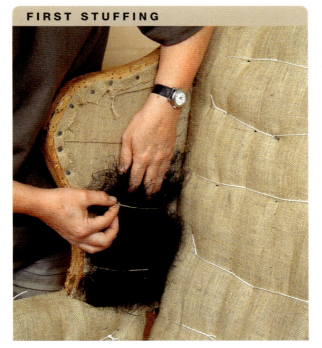

4 Carry out the first stuffing to the back, arms and seat of the chair before stuffing the wings. Stitch stuffing ties over the surface of the hessian covering the wings and stuff with fibre.

SECOND HESSIAN LAYER

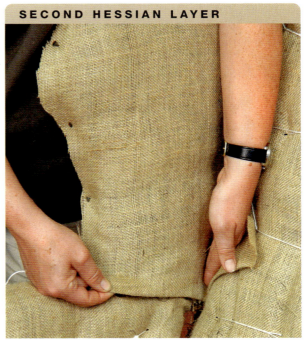

5 Cover the stuffing with hessian. Temporarily tack the hessian along the top and front edge of the wing frame and then fold the bottom edge under where it joins the top of the arm. Make any appropriate cuts to the back edge of the hessian so that it fits around the frame and then tuck it through the gap between the back frame and wing webbing.

SECOND HESSIAN LAYER

6 Pull the back edge of the hessian through the gap between the wing webbing and back frame and pull it tight to shape the stuffing. Use upholstery skewers to hold the back edge of the hessian in place and replace the temporary tacks on the top and front edges of the wing frame with permanent ones, smoothing the hessian over the stuffing as you go.

SECOND HESSIAN LAYER

7 Smooth the hessian on the inside wing down towards the bottom edge and, using a curved needle and twine, stitch it in place where it joins the hessian covering the first stuffing on the arm.

Wing chair

SECOND HESSIAN LAYER

8 Once you have stitched the bottom edge of the wing hessian to the top of the arm, remove the upholstery skewers and pull the back edge of the hessian around the wing webbing, towards the front of the chair.

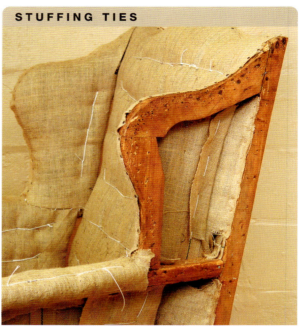
STUFFING TIES

9 Hold the back edge of the hessian in place with skewers if necessary and stitch a line of through-stuffing ties through the back edge of the wing to firm up the stuffing and secure the back edge of the hessian to the wing webbing.

SECOND STUFFING

10 Carry out a second stuffing on the seat, back, arms and, finally, wings. Secure the calico to the out-facing sides of the wing frames and skewer the back edge around the wing webbing so that it's held out of the way while you put the top fabric on the back of the chair. Fold the bottom edge of the wing calico under so that it forms a neat join between the wing and the arm.

COVERING INSIDE BACK

11 Apply the top fabric to the inside back of the chair first over a layer of wadding and fleece. Cut into the outside edges of the back fabric so that it fits around the frame and pull it through the gap between the webbing at the back of the wing and the back frame. Tack the fabric in place around the back of the frame.

120 APPLYING BASIC SKILLS

COVERING INSIDE ARMS

12 Apply top fabric to the inside arms over a layer of wadding and fleece. Tack the arm fabric to the arm and back frames and leave 2.5 cm (1 in) of excess where the arm fabric meets the bottom panel of the wing.

> 📖 **Tip**
>
> It's easy to get too close to your work – stand back from the chair and check that the arms and wings are the same each side.

PIPING

13 Make a length of piping sufficient for both wings (see Basic Upholstery Techniques, page 25). Take half the piping and run it from the back frame, level with the arm, around the bottom of the wing where it joins the arm, and under the arm frame. Check that the piping is straight and positioned where you want the join between arm and wing to be and then tack one end to the back frame and the other to the underside of the arm frame. Pull the excess arm fabric up underneath the piping and pin it in place.

PADDING INSIDE WING

14 Cover the inside of the wing with a layer of wadding. Cover the wadding with a layer of synthetic fleece and tack it all around to hold the wadding in place.

11 Wing chair

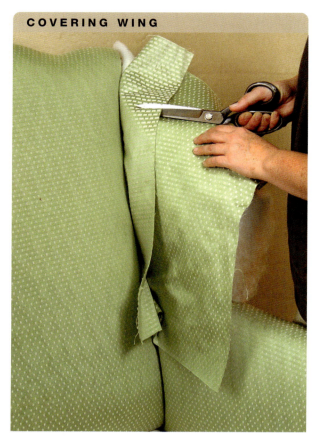

15 Apply the top fabric to the wing. Make cuts to the back edge of the fabric and tuck it through the gap between the back and the wing webbing.

16 Skewer the back edge of the wing fabric to hold it in place while you smooth the rest of the wing fabric around the top and front edges of the wing frame and tack to the outside edge of the wing frame.

17 Fold the bottom edge of the wing fabric under so that it makes a neat join with the piping pinned to the top of the arm. With a curved needle and thread, carefully hand stitch the wing and arm fabric together through the piping so that all three are pulled together invisibly.

122 APPLYING BASIC SKILLS

COVERING WING

18 Remove the skewers from the back edge of the wing fabric and tack it to the back frame. Then do the same with the calico that was skewered out of the way in step 10.

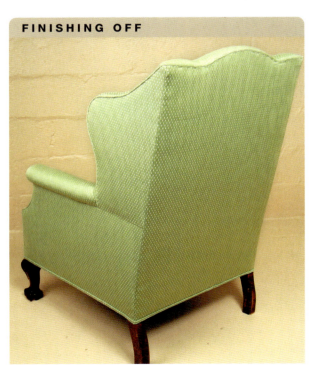

FINISHING OFF

19 Apply the seat fabric and finish off by covering the outside arms, wings and back. When a seat has a cushion you can save fabric by using calico under the portion of the seat that doesn't show.

Top Piped edges aren't essential but they invariably finish things off with style.
Above Use a paper template to get the exact shape of the seat and use it to cut out the top and bottom pieces of your seat cushion.

12 Tub chair

The challenge presented by tub chairs, from an upholsterer's point of view, are the two curves that make them look so beautiful. The inside of the chair sweeps around from scroll to scroll and the tops of the arms invariably flow down gracefully from the peak of the back. The approach to a tub chair, because the arms and back are one piece, is exactly the same as that employed when upholstering a chesterfield. Like a chesterfield, the back and arms of a tub chair can be buttoned or left plain. When buttoned, the joins in the fabric are hidden within the folds between the buttons so that it looks as if it's covered using one piece. When upholstering without buttons, as shown here, the join between arms and back is assisted with piping.

tools

Wooden mallet

Tack lifter

Pincers

Knife

Scissors

Webbing stretcher

Magnetic tack hammer

13 cm (5 in) spring needle

30 cm (12 in) double-ended needle

Stuffing regulator

Upholstery skewers

Curved hand-stitching needle

materials

Webbing

13 mm (½ in) and 10 mm (⅜ in) upholstery tacks

Springs

Flax twine

Lay cord

Hessian

Vegetable fibre

Calico

Wadding

Synthetic fleece

Top fabric

Cotton thread

Piping cord

 key skills

You will gain experience of upholstering arms and the back as one piece and also how to align and keep fabric smooth over a double curved surface.

12 Tub chair

STRIPPING

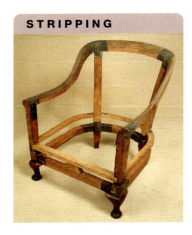

WEBBING

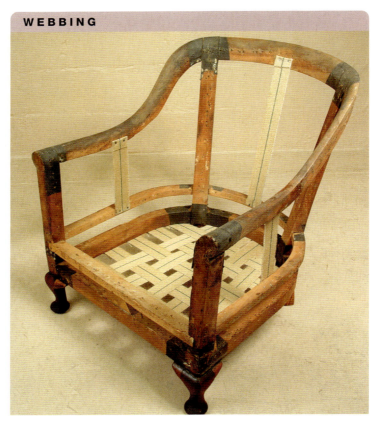

> **Tip**
>
> On a tub chair you'll give yourself more room to work and find it easier if you completely finish the back and arms first before springing the seat.

1 Strip off all existing upholstery (see Basic Upholstery Techniques, pages 14–15). Leave any seat springs attached to their webbing if possible, to remind you of their positioning when you come to put them back.

2 Re-web the seat (see Basic Upholstery Techniques, page 16). Attach strips of webbing between the top and bottom rungs of the arms and back. This webbing is simply added to support the hessian in step 3.

FIRST HESSIAN LAYER

FIRST STUFFING

3 Cover the inside arms and back with hessian.

4 Stitch stuffing ties around the inside of the chair and stuff with an even layer of fibre.

SECOND HESSIAN LAYER

5 Cut out a piece of hessian to cover the stuffing on the inside back of the chair and another piece each for the arms. Make sure that all the pieces will overlap. Place the back hessian over the inside back and make cuts into the bottom edge.

SECOND HESSIAN LAYER

6 Bring the bottom edge of the hessian under the bottom frame rail and tack in place.

SECOND HESSIAN LAYER

7 Using the heel of your free hand, smooth the hessian up from the bottom and over the top of the chair back, and tack in place. Once you have secured the back hessian, do the same with the arm pieces, making cuts to the top and bottom of the hessian at intervals so that it fits tightly to the curves of the frame.

SECOND HESSIAN LAYER

8 Tack the front edge of the arm hessian to the scrolls (see steps 7–9, project 10, page 111 for details).

SECOND HESSIAN LAYER

9 To form a neat join between the inside back and arm hessian, make cuts into the overlapping edges to allow the hessian to follow the inner curve of the tub, and fold the edges under. Hold the join together with upholstery skewers while you stitch the join using flax twine and a spring needle.

12 Tub chair

REGULATING STUFFING

10 Regulate the stuffing to eliminate any lumps and fill the scroll edges with fibre. Stitch edge rolls around the scrolls and through stuffing ties on the inside of the tub to compact the stuffing. (See steps 13–15, project 3 pages 54–55 for details.)

SECOND STUFFING

11 Carry out a second stuffing and cover with calico as you did the hessian in steps 5–9. Apply a layer of wadding and synthetic fleece to hold it in place.

TOP FABRIC

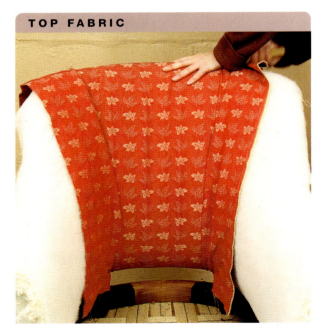

12 Take the back fabric and attach it to the inside back in exactly the same way as you did the hessian in steps 5–7. Take time to align any pattern and make sure that it's the right way up.

TOP FABRIC

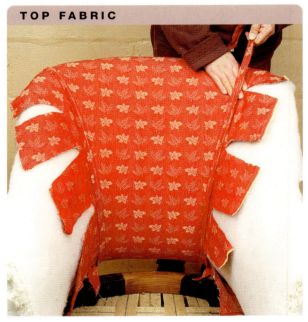

13 The joins between the back and arm fabric will be piped, so decide where they will be and attach the piping to the underside of the chair and over the top of the frame so it lies flat against the inside back fabric.

128 APPLYING BASIC SKILLS

14 Cut into the edges of the top fabric up to the piping and skewer the piping in place making sure that the flange of the piping faces out towards the front of the arms.

15 Lay the fabric over the arms and ensure that the pattern is straight and matches the pattern on the inside back. When you're happy with the positioning of the fabric, attach it as you did the hessian and calico. Cut into the back edge of the fabric where it overlaps the back fabric and fold under so that it makes a join along the piping. Skewer the join together and carefully hand stitch the fabric and piping in place. See Basic Upholstery Techniques, page 24.

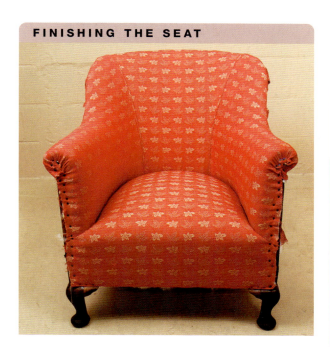

16 Once the back and arms are finished spring, stuff and cover the seat.

Above You can't expect to match a fabric pattern up on a surface like this, but it will look fine as long as the pattern is straight.

12 Tub chair

ADDING PIPING

17 Attach piping all around the top of the outside arms and back, from the underneath of one scroll to the other.

COVERING OUTSIDE SURFACES

18 Fill the outside arms and back with calico and synthetic fleece. Position and secure the top fabric under the seat frame and cut and fold the top edge so that it makes a join with the piping and skewer in place.

COVERING OUTSIDE SURFACES

19 Stitch the inside and outside fabric to the piping and the join between outside back and outside arms.

> **Tip**
> When you finish an edge with piping, always keep joins and ends smooth by peeling back the fabric and trimming off unwanted piping cord.

Right Tub chairs are a mass of curves – challenging but rewarding to upholster.

130 APPLYING BASIC SKILLS

FINISHING SCROLLS

20 Frame the scrolls by tacking a length of piping around the edge of the scrolls.

FINISHING SCROLLS

21 Fill the inside of the piped scroll with some teased-out cotton wadding.

FINISHING SCROLLS

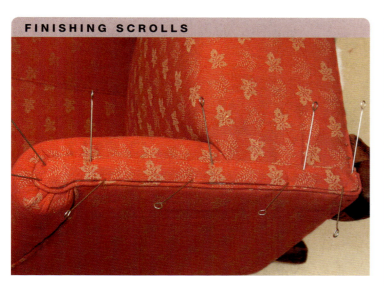

22 Shape and skewer a piece of fabric to the inside of the piped scrolls. Make sure that the scroll fabric lines up with the pattern on the inside arms and front fabric, and then stitch in place.

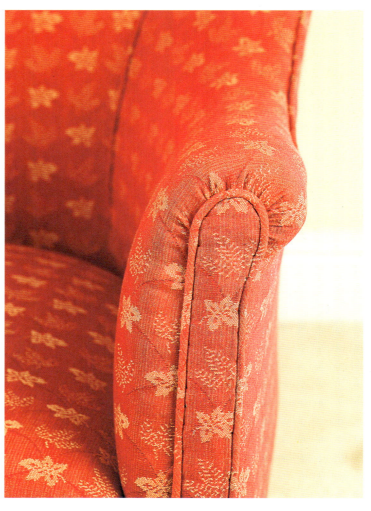

Right With a bit of practice, hand stitching a scroll doesn't take too long and the result is a professional finish to the front of the arm and chair.

13 Chaise longue

The approach to take with a chaise longue is to upholster it as if it is a one-armed chair with a long seat. The seat is a sprung, overstuffed base. The hump is the same as an arm with springs on the top and inside face, and the back rest is a pin-cushion pad. You can button all of the upholstery or leave it plain. The chaise in this example has beautiful, carved show wood along the back and on the front of the hump. This example has a buttoned back and hump, but a plain seat.

tools

Wooden mallet

Tack lifter

Pincers

Knife

Scissors

Webbing stretcher

Magnetic tack hammer

13 cm (5 in) spring needle

30 cm (12 in) double-ended needle

Stuffing regulator

Upholstery skewers

Curved hand-stitching needle

materials

Webbing

13 mm (½ in) and 10 mm (⅜ in) upholstery tacks

Springs

Flax and buttoning twine

Lay cord

Hessian

Vegetable fibre

Calico

Wadding

Synthetic fleece

Top fabric

Covered buttons

Cotton thread

Double piping cord, decorative cord or braiding

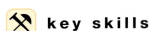 key skills

Deep buttoning a curved surface working tightly against show wood is introduced in this project.

13 Chaise longue

STRIPPING

1 Strip off all existing upholstery (see Basic Upholstery Techniques, pages 14–15). Save the springs, any good-quality horsehair and check the frame for damage. If your chaise has show wood, now is a good time to give it a wax, but make sure you polish it all off before applying any expensive fabric.

WEBBING

2 Re-web (see Basic Upholstery Techniques, page 16), spring (see page 17), and complete the first and second stuffings on the seat and hump (see pages 22–23). Treat the back rest as an upholstered pad with just one stuffing. Cover all stuffed surfaces with calico. Decide how many buttons you want and use upholstery skewers to mark their positions provisionally.

BUTTON POSITIONS

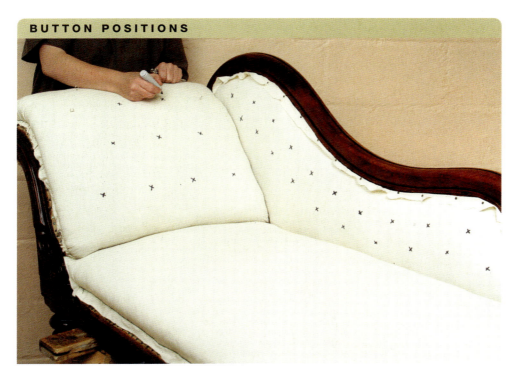

3 Finalize the button positions by measuring, and replace the skewers with marker pen crosses.

134 APPLYING BASIC SKILLS

BUTTON POSITIONS

BUTTONING BACK REST

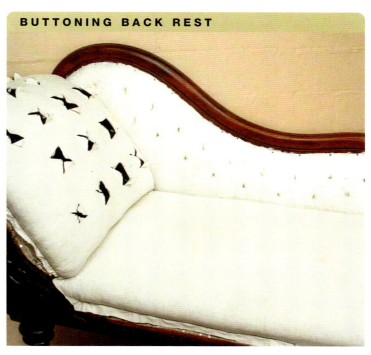

4 Cut into each of the button positions down to, but not through, the first layer of hessian.

> 📖 **Tip**
>
> If possible, always make a record of the original button positions so that they can be transferred to the new upholstery.

5 Button the back rest first. Cover the pad with a layer of wadding and then synthetic fleece to hold the wadding in place. Tack the top edge of the fleece in place with a few 10 mm (⅜ in) tacks and tuck through where it meets the hump and seat. Feel through the fleece and wadding and reopen the button positions with your fingers.

BUTTONING BACK REST

6 The back rest has only one stuffing and is an example of pin-cushion upholstery shown in project 2 (see pages 42–49). Buttoning the back rest is straightforward: (see steps 15–21, project 5, pages 71–73 for details). When you come to attach the top edge of the fabric, make vertical folds up from the buttons and tack in place along the edge of the show wood.

13 Chaise longue

TRIMMING TOP FABRIC

7 Once all the buttoning has been done, and the top edge has been tacked in place, carefully trim the fabric along the line of the show wood.

Above Make all folds face downwards so that they don't trap dust.

BUTTONING HUMP

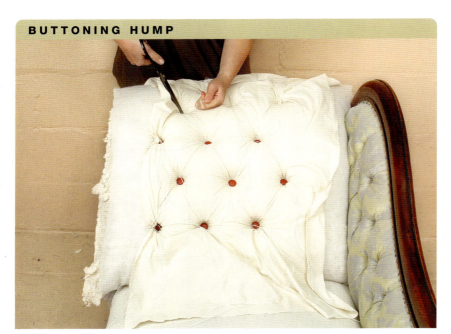

BUTTONING HUMP

8 The hump has two stuffings and so the buttons will be deeper than those on the back rest. You may be using an expensive fabric, which leaves no room for error with the button positions. Therefore, button a piece of calico in place first as if it were the top fabric. Make all the adjustments you need until the calico is buttoned to your satisfaction and then remove it and use as a template for transferring the button positions on to the top fabric. Place a small stitch in coloured cotton to mark each button position – don't risk using pen or any other marker.

9 Start with the bottom row of buttons and work your way up, folding the fabric as you go (see steps 15–21, project 5, pages 71–73 for details).

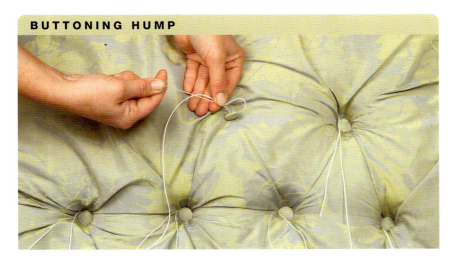

BUTTONING HUMP

10 When access behind a piece is limited, you will find it difficult to pass the double-ended needle all the way through and out of the back – here's a way around the problem. Take the middle of a length of twine and thread the loop through the needle about 5 cm (2 in), and push the threaded end through first until the twine emerges from the back of the upholstery. Pass a piece of webbing under the twine loop and then, carefully, pull the needle out of the front again and off the twine. Thread a button onto the twine and tie both ends with a slipknot. Pull up on the knot and push the button down into the hole.

BUTTONING HUMP

11 When you've got all your buttons in place, make sure they're all adjusted to the same depth and that your folds are neat.

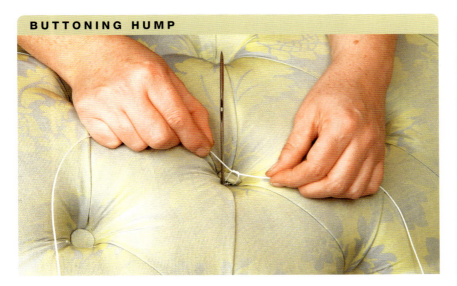

BUTTONING HUMP

12 When you're happy with the buttoning, push the needle down through the buttonhole so that the eye end protrudes and lifts the button a little. Tie three ordinary knots down into the button to tie it off. Thread the twine in the needle and pull the needle out at the back of the hump, so that the twine is pulled into the buttonhole.

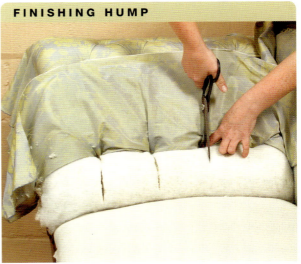

FINISHING HUMP

13 Lift up the bottom edge of the fabric and make straight cuts down from each of the bottom-row buttons, through the fleece, wadding and calico. This is to allow the folds from the bottom-row buttons to lie flat.

> **Tip**
>
> Always be prepared to make adjustments to your button positions as you work – a curved surface will nearly always require some adjustments.

CHAISE LONGUE

13 Chaise longue

FINISHING HUMP

14 Make the bottom edge folds, tuck the fabric through and tack under the bottom rung of the hump frame.

Above Make sure that any tacks holding the top fabric in place will be hidden by your trimming.

FINISHING HUMP

15 Make folds from each row of buttons out to the show-wood scroll. Tack in place and trim the fabric tight to the edge of the show wood.

Above Polish show wood first – before upholstering.

FINISHING BACK REST

16 At the back of the back rest, tie off each button's twine to a tack on the frame.

COVERING SEAT

17 Now, cover the seat and trim off the fabric tight to the show wood. Expensive shears earn their keep with jobs like this.

COVERING SEAT

18 Finish the edges of fabric and show wood with double piping glued in place, or decorative cord stitched in place.

FINISHING OFF

19 Finish the underside of the hump in exactly the same way as the outside arm on a chair (see steps 17–19, project 10, pages 113–114 for details). Finally, finish the outside back by attaching piping to the top edge, tacking the fabric under the bottom rail, and hand stitching the top edge of the fabric to the piping.

CHAISE LONGUE 139

14 Drop-arm sofa

Drop-arm sofas have one arm that is attached to the seat by a hinged mechanism that allows it to be lowered from the upright position to flat or somewhere between the two. The secret to upholstering a drop-arm sofa is to make it look like an ordinary sofa when the arm is in the upright position and not to allow the arm upholstery to sag when lowered. Also, care must be taken in the early stages of reupholstery to ensure that the arm's movement does not damage any of the seat springs.

tools

Wooden mallet

Tack lifter

Pincers

Knife

Scissors

Screwdriver

Webbing stretcher

Magnetic tack hammer

13 cm (5 in) spring needle

30 cm (12 in) double-ended needle

Stuffing regulator

Upholstery skewers

Curved hand-stitching needle

Tape measure

materials

Webbing

13 mm (½ in) and 10 mm (⅜ in) upholstery tacks

Springs

Flax twine

Lay cord

Cane

Hessian

Vegetable fibre

Calico

Wadding

Synthetic fleece

Top fabric

Cotton thread

Piping cord

key skills

Learn how to upholster and cover an arm that will move against and fit tight to other surfaces.

14 Drop-arm sofa

STRIPPING

1 Strip off the existing upholstery (see Basic Upholstery Techniques, pages 14–15). Pay careful attention to how the drop arm fits and note the seat spring positions at the drop-arm end. It's important that you put them back, so that the arm doesn't touch them when lowered. Remove the drop arm during the stripping process and then replace it once stripped. Use new screws to attach it to the hinges.

WEBBING

2 Re-web the seat and back (see Basic Upholstery Techniques, page 16). Check the old springs and replace any that are broken or don't compress evenly, replace the old front edge cane if broken. Re-spring the seat and back, and cover with hessian – note that the sofa shown doesn't have back springs.

STUFFING

3 Carry out the first and second stuffings on the fixed arm and back, and the first stuffing of the seat. When stuffing the seat, ensure that it's level along the front and also where it meets the drop arm. Stitch an edge roll along the front and where the seat meets the drop arm (see step 12, project 3, page 54 for details).

STUFFING

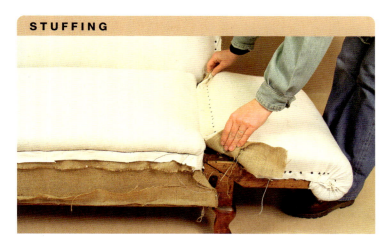

4 Carry out a second stuffing of the seat and a first and second stuffing of the drop arm. Upholster the drop arm while it's attached to the sofa so that you can compare it with the fixed arm and to ensure that it doesn't interfere with the back or seat when raised and lowered. When you upholster the drop arm, ensure that you leave access to the hinges securing it to the sofa.

COVERING INSIDE SURFACES

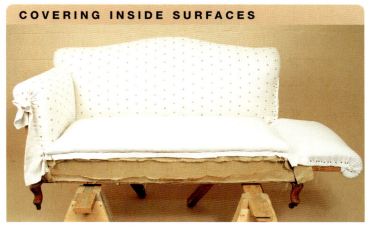

5 Cover the sofa back and inside fixed arm with top fabric.

COVERING DROP ARM

6 Put the drop arm in the upright position while you're covering it and make sure that you position the fabric so that it matches the back and fixed arm.

COVERING DROP ARM

7 Carefully unscrew the drop arm and remove it. Make sure you use a clean screwdriver.

COVERING DROP ARM

8 Attach a piece of fabric to the inside area of the sofa back where it meets the back scroll of the drop arm. Use skewers to hold the fabric in the appropriate shape and then hand stitch in place, using a curved hand-stitching needle.

> **Tip**
>
> Make sure you understand how the drop-arm mechanism works and its range of movement before reupholstering.

14 Drop-arm sofa

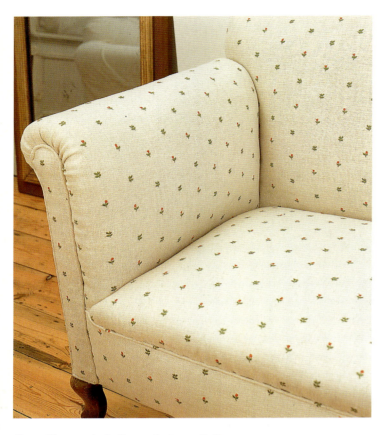

Above Aim to make both arms look exactly the same.

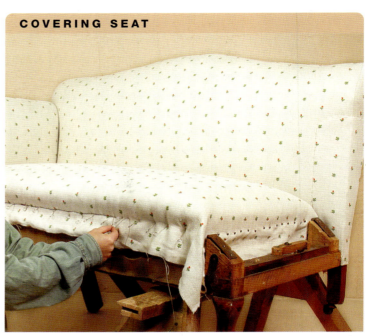

COVERING SEAT

9 Attach the top fabric to the seat. Stitch the fabric to the edge where it meets the drop arm, leaving enough excess fabric to attach to the bottom of the arm later.

FINISHING DROP ARM

10 With the drop arm removed, skewer the top fabric in place and stitch to the scroll end that rests against the inside back of the sofa. Make an unpiped scroll for the back end of the arm and allow excess fabric to fold around the outside arm and attach to the seat.

FINISHING DROP ARM

11 Now skewer the top fabric to the outside arm fabric and stitch to the underside of the arm roll.

FINISHING DROP ARM

12 Carefully put the drop arm back in position and screw it securely to the hinges.

FINISHING DROP ARM

13 Put the arm in the upright position and attach two lengths of folded webbing, on the outside face, between the arm and the base of the sofa, one at the front and one at the back. This webbing is to prevent the arm from going past the upright position and will form firm edges where there's no frame. Make sure the folded edge points outwards.

FINISHING DROP ARM

14 Fold the rear scroll fabric around the back edge of the drop arm. Secure it to the sofa and arm frames with tacks, and stitch it to the webbing that forms an edge between the two.

FINISHING DROP ARM

15 The drop arm on this sofa is operated by a mechanism that you pull with a cord. Make a neat hole in an appropriate place for the cord to come through and stitch the edges to neaten it.

14 Drop-arm sofa

Left and above Drop arms are fine for supporting feet but are not designed for sitting on.

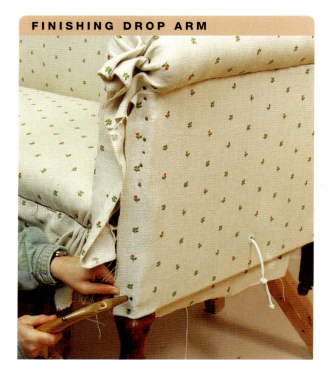

FINISHING DROP ARM

16 Once you've ensured that the arm mechanism can be operated with the outside arm fabric in place, secure it in position under the seat frame and around the webbed front edge.

FINISHING DROP ARM

17 Tack the outside arm fabric where you can to hold it in place and then carefully stitch it to the edge webbing.

146 APPLYING BASIC SKILLS

FINISHING FRONT EDGE

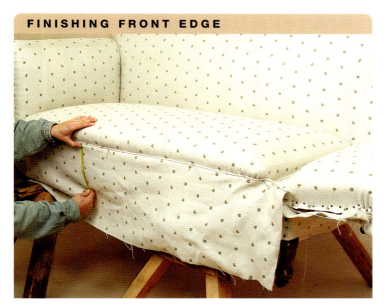

18 Make up a piece of fabric to cover the front edge by sewing a length of piping along its top edge and then skewer it in position. Before you hand stitch it in place measure to check that you have it on straight.

FINISHING FRONT EDGE

19 Stuff underneath the front edge and attach the fabric under the seat frame.

FINISHING ARM SCROLLS

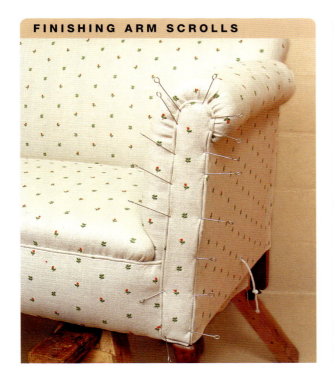

20 Attach the outside arm fabric to the fixed arm and finish off both arm scrolls by skewering a length of piping to the appropriate shape, filling with fabric over a little cotton wadding and hand stitching to the arm.

FINISHING OFF

21 Drop the arm to its lowest position and carefully stitch the seat fabric across the gap to the underside of the arm. Cover the outside back and attach a bottom cloth.

15 Buttoned leather chesterfield

This Victorian chesterfield sofa is covered in ruby-red leather. With slight alterations, the procedures below apply equally to the use of any fabric. If you want to upholster your chesterfield in fabric without buttons, apply the same principles used for upholstering the tub chair in project 12 (see pages 124–131). The use of leather, however, requires the buttoning of the back and arms, as you won't be able to hand stitch the join between the two. If using leather, leave the seat free of upholstery until the back and arms are finished: manipulating leather is hard work, made harder if you have to lean over a built-up seat.

tools

Wooden mallet
Tack lifter
Pincers
Knife
Scissors
Webbing stretcher
Magnetic tack hammer
13 cm (5 in) spring needle
30 cm (12 in) double-ended needle
Stuffing regulator
Metre rule
Tape measure
Upholstery skewers
Marker pen
Curved hand-stitching needle

materials

Webbing
13 mm (½ in) and 10 mm (⅜ in) upholstery tacks
Springs
Flax twine
Lay cord
Cane
Hessian
Vegetable fibre
Calico
Wadding
Synthetic fleece
Cotton thread
Top fabric
Covered buttons
Dome-headed upholstery nails
Piping cord

key skills

To complete this project you will learn how to do deep buttoning and how to hide the join between the back and arms. You will also gain experience of working with leather and close nailing.

15 Buttoned leather chesterfield

STRIPPING

1 Strip off all existing upholstery (see Basic Upholstery Techniques, pages 14–15). Take your time and leave the back springs and webbing until last. Make a note of, or sketch, the spring positions and cut the webbing away panel by panel leaving the springs attached to the webbing. Then replace the webbing and stitch the springs back where they came from.

FIRST HESSIAN LAYER

2 Cover the springs with hessian and stitch the tops in place. Cut the hessian to the same width for the back and arms – it needs to be even. You may find that raising the sofa onto sturdy trestles makes certain jobs easier.

FIRST STUFFING

3 Stuff the back and arms, stitch edge rolls to the scrolls and through-stuffing ties around the inside and top of the arms and back (see steps 13–15, project 3, pages 54–55 for details). Use one piece of hessian for the inside back and a piece each for the arms. Make and stitch the joins between the back and arms as for the tub chair (see step 9, project 12, page 127 for detail).

150 APPLYING BASIC SKILLS

SECOND STUFFING

BUTTON POSITIONS

4 After a second stuffing you're ready to mark out the button positions. Work out how many rows of buttons you want and then use the floor and a metre rule to mark the bottom line of the bottom buttons, and work up from that.

5 Use a tape measure to position the buttons along the horizontal. Place upholstery skewers where you think the buttons should go and make any adjustments before marking the button positions with crosses in marker pen.

BUTTON POSITIONS

6 Cut into each of the button positions, through both layers of stuffing and up to, but not through, the first layer of hessian over the springs.

BUTTON POSITIONS

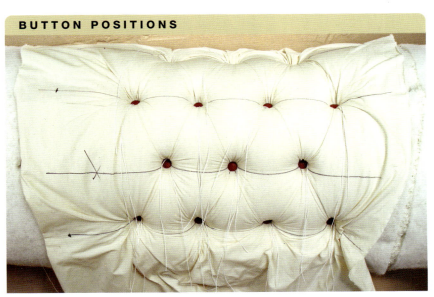

7 Cover the inside back and arms with a layer of wadding and synthetic fleece to hold it in place and then re-excavate the buttonholes through the wadding. Take a piece of calico and button it to the back as if it were the top cover (see step 8, project 13, page 136 for details). Make any adjustments to the button positions at this stage.

BUTTONED LEATHER CHESTERFIELD 151

15 Buttoned leather chesterfield

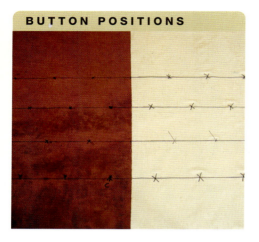

BUTTON POSITIONS

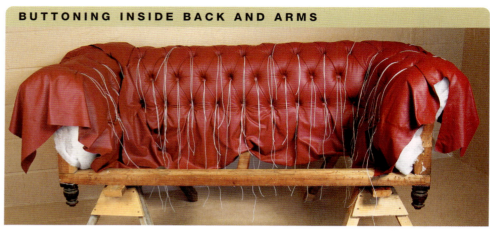

BUTTONING INSIDE BACK AND ARMS

8 Remove the buttoned calico and use it as a template to mark the button positions on to the three pieces of hide that will cover the back and arms.

9 It's often difficult to pull the buttoning needle out of the back of a curved area so it may be easier to button the leather to the back and arms with the twine exiting from the front (see step 10, project 13, page 137 for details.

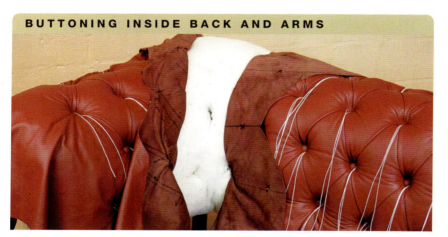

BUTTONING INSIDE BACK AND ARMS

10 Where the inside back meets the arms, button the back right up to the corner, remove the buttons and fold the fabric back out of the way. Then do the same with the leather on the arm so that the overlapping button positions are shown on each piece.

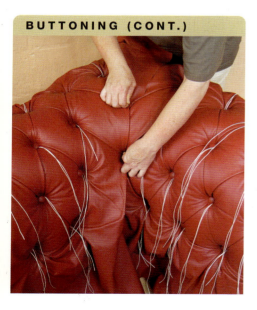

BUTTONING (CONT.)

11 Relocate the overlapping button in both arm and back pieces so that the two ride over the top of each other and the folds form a seamless joint.

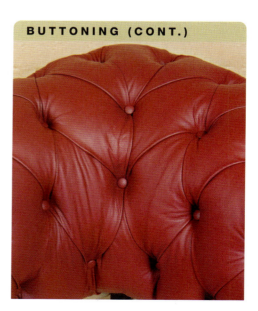

BUTTONING (CONT.)

12 When the buttoning is finished the back and arms should look as if they are covered using one piece of hide.

Above There are few things more impressive in upholstery than top-quality, deep-buttoned leather.

BUTTONING SEAT

13 Re-web, spring and stuff the seat in exactly the same way as the seat on the Art Deco armchair (see steps 5–13, project 9, pages 103–105 for details). Cover the seat with a layer each of wadding and synthetic fleece. Taking your lead from the button positions on the inside back and arms, mark out where you want the buttons on the seat to go, using upholstery skewers.

BUTTONING SEAT

14 Finalize the button positions and excavate each one through both layers of stuffing. Cover with a layer of wadding and synthetic fleece to hold it in place as you did in steps 6 and 7.

15 Buttoned leather chesterfield

COVERING SEAT

15 Make up the hide for the seat: stitch "fly pieces" of hessian to the back and sides of the hide. (Fly pieces are used so that you don't waste expensive fabric where it's not needed or seen.) Then stitch a second piece of leather along the front edge of the seat hide.

Use piping to conceal the join and stitch folded panels into the leather as you go. Button the seat in the usual way and then tack the back and sides in position and skewer the front piece in place so that the piping runs just under the caned edge of the chesterfield.

COVERING SEAT

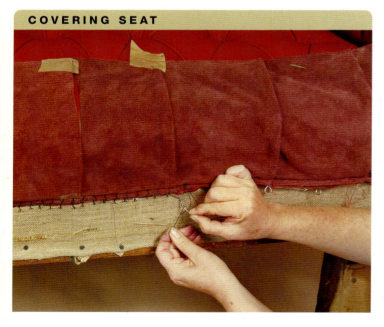

16 Stitch the join between the front and seat leather in position just under the edge cane using buttoning twine or strong thread.

COVERING SEAT

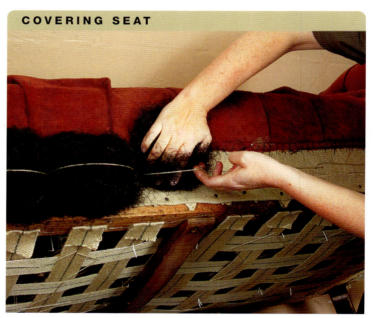

17 Stuff underneath the front piece and tack in place under the seat frame.

 Tip

Because the front edge has decorative buttons you'll need to pad it with more stuffing than usual.

FINISHING OFF

18 Sew a button slightly more than halfway up each of the creases. Pull the twine through, making sure you don't snag any springs, and attach it to a tack under the front seat rail.

FINISHING OFF

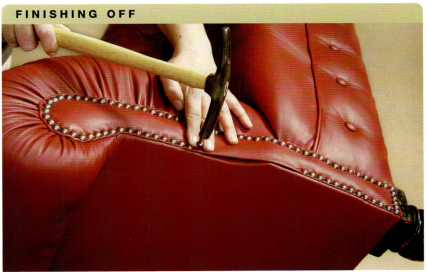

19 Attach the outside back and side pieces and finish the scrolls in the usual way (see steps 20–21, project 10, page 114 for details), but edge with dome-headed upholstery nails (see steps 16–18, project 2, pages 48–49 for details). Go slowly and use your fingers to judge an even distance between the heads.

Left If you use the best leather your hard work will last longer than a lifetime.

BUTTONED LEATHER CHESTERFIELD 155

Glossary

Bergère Style of chair or sofa where the arms and back flow into one another. In modern usage usually refers to a sofa or chair with caned panels filling the arms or back, or both.

Bottom cloth Piece of fabric, usually hessian or black calico, attached under the seat of a chair or sofa to cover the seat webbing and prevent dust falling from the upholstery.

Braid Woven decorative trimming used to finish off edges and cover tack heads.

Buttoning needle See double-ended needle.

Calico Plain white or unbleached cotton fabric. Also known as muslin.

Cambric Similar to calico fabric but with a glaze on one side, used as a feather-proof casing.

Deep buttoning Method of buttoning fabric that creates a surface covered with buttons, with patterned folds between them.

Double-ended needle Long needle with one eye and a point at each end. Used where it's necessary to stitch through stuffing. For example, stitching through stuffing ties, edge rolls and attaching buttons.

Edge roll The edge of a stuffed pad that has been stitched to firm and shape it.

Flax twine Thin, rough twine made from natural vegetable fibre.

Fly piece Strip of hessian or scrap of fabric sewn to the edge of inside arms, backs or seat fabric where it doesn't show to economize on top fabric.

Gimp Woven decorative trimming used to finish off edges and cover tack heads.

Gimp pins Thin upholstery tacks in various colours for attaching gimp and other trimmings.

Hessian Strong, plain weaved fabric made from natural vegetable fibre. Also known as burlap or sack cloth. Good quality hessian is often referred to as tarpaulin or scrim.

Interliner Fire-retardant cloth, similar to calico, used to cover upholstery before applying non-fire-retardant top fabric.

Jute Rough fibre made from the bark of the jute plant. Used for making twine and rope, and woven into hessian, sacking and mats.

Linseed oil Natural oil used to treat and preserve wooden tools.

Lay cord Cord or string made out of flax or jute. Also called laid cord.

Loose cover A cover made of fabric to lay directly over a sofa or chair without being secured. Also known as a slip cover.

Mallet Wooden hammer used for striking another tool, such as a tack lifter, and used where damage would be caused with an ordinary, metal-headed hammer.

Magnetic tack hammer Small-headed hammer with a magnetized end for picking up and holding tacks for one-handed tasks.

Nap The direction in which the weave of a fabric runs. Going with the nap the fabric is smooth; going against it it is rough.

Netting staples U-shaped pieces of galvanised wire with a sharp point on each end. In upholstery these are used to attach springs to wooden chairs and sofa frames.

Pin-cushion upholstery Type of thin upholstery pad, likened to a pin cushion because it has no raised edge.

Regulating To even out stuffing using a regulator.

Regulator Strong, eyeless needle of varying lengths – between 5–30 cm (2–12 in) used to distribute stuffing once it has been covered.

Stuffing Vegetable fibre or horsehair used as the main filling of upholstery.

Stuffing regulator See regulator.

Spring needle A large, curved upholstery needle with a dagger point used to stitch through hessian with twine. Used, amongst other things, for stitching the tops of springs to hessian and their bases to webbing.

Stuffing ties Large loop stitches of twine under which stuffing is tucked to hold it in place.

Tack lifter Tool used to lever tacks out of wood.

Tacking strip Thin strip of often vulcanised card used when attaching outside arms and backs to leave a straight invisible join.

Through stuffing ties Twine stitches that go all the way through a stuffed pad to compact or shape the stuffing within it.

Van Dyke join Method of joining two pieces of fabric when deep buttoning so that the join is hidden by folds between the buttons.

Wadding Compressed cotton felt used as a smoothing layer underneath top fabric.

Whipping A method of attaching cane to springs along the front edge of a chair or sofa seat using a succession of tied twine loops. Can also be referred to as lashing.

Webbing Strong woven fabric strips usually between 5–7.5 cm (2–3 in) wide, often made of flax and attached to the wooden furniture frame to support upholstery.

Webbing stretcher Tool used to apply tension to webbing while it's being attached to the wooden furniture frame.

Suppliers

UNITED KINGDOM

FABRIC

G.P. & J. Baker
G.P. & J Baker House
6 Stinsford Road
Poole
Dorset
BH17 0SW
Tel: 01202 266700
www.gpjbaker.com

Crowson
Crowson House
Bellbrook Park
Uckfield
East Sussex
TN22 1QZ
Tel: 01825 761055
E-mail: sales@crowsonfabrics.com
www.crowsonfabrics.com

Fabric World
6-10 Brighton Road
South Croydon
CR2 6AA
Tel: 020 86886282
— and —
287–289 High Street
Sutton
Surrey
SM1 1LL
Tel: 020 86435127
E-mail: info@fabricworldlondon.co.uk
www.fabricworldlondon.co.uk

Fired Earth
Fired Earth Interiors
Twyford Mill
Oxford Road
Adderbury
Oxfordshire
OX17 3SX
Tel: 01295 814300
www.firedearth.com

Monkwell
Bellbrook Park
Uckfield
East Sussex
TN22 1HW
Tel: 01825 747901
E-mail: enquiries@monkwell.com
www.monkwell.com

LEATHER

Andrew Muirhead & Son Ltd
Dalmarnock Leather Works
273-289 Dunn Street
Glasgow
Scotland
G40 3EA
Tel: 0141 5543724
E-mail: sales@muirhead.co.uk
www.muirhead.co.uk

TOOLS ETC.

oldsofas
Gwenlais House
Pentregwenlais
Llandybie
Carmarthenshire
SA18 3JH
Tel: 01269 820009
E-mail: david@oldsofas.com
www.oldsofas.com

SOUTH AFRICA

Cape Town

Kehl's Upholstery Supplies
403 Voortrekker Road
Maitland
7405
Tel: 021 511 2061
Fax: 021 511 4220
E-mail: kehl@kehls.co.za
Suppliers of fabrics, trimmings and tools

U&G Fabrics – Upholstery and General
14 Bella Rosa Street
Rosenpark
Bellville
7530
Tel: 021 914 8180
Fax: 021 914 8182
E-mail: admin@ugfabrics.co.za
www.upholsteryandgeneral.co.za
Suppliers of fabrics, trimmings and tools

U&G Fabrics – Upholstery and General
Shop 25, The Palms
145 Sir Lowry Road
Woodstock
7925
Tel: 021 462 5898
Fax: 021 462 5892
E-mail: admin@ugfabrics.co.za
www.upholsteryandgeneral.co.za
Suppliers of fabrics, trimmings and tools

Durban

Classic Textiles
126 Archary Rd
Clairwood
Durban
4052
Tel: 031 465 9016
Fax: 031 465 9003
E-mail: info@classictextiles.co.za

U&G Fabrics – Upholstery and General
130 Brickfield Road
Overport
4091
Durban
Tel: 031 209 3166
Fax: 031 208 0565
E-mail: admin@ugfabrics.co.za
www.upholsteryandgeneral.co.za
Suppliers of fabrics, trimmings and tools

Gauteng

Fabric & Decor
Shop 22, Town Square
Weltevreden Park
Roodepoort
1709
Tel: 011 675 2135
Fax: 011 675 1246

U&G Fabrics – Upholstery and General
324 Old Pretoria Road
Midrand
1685
Tel: 011 315 3157
Fax: 011 315 7392
E-mail: admin@ugfabrics.co.za
www.upholsteryandgeneral.co.za
Suppliers of fabrics, trimmings and tools

G.U.S General Upholstery Suppliers (Pty) Ltd
131 Pritchard Street
Johannesburg
2000
Tel: 011 337 4947
Fax: 011 333 5224

Pretoria

Home Hyper City
19 Pretorius Street
Pretoria
0001
Tel: 012 323 7860
Fax: 012 325 4936
E-mail: carrim@pixie.co.za

Bloemfontein

U&G Fabrics – Upholstery and General
103 Kellner Street
Westdene
Bloemfontein
9310
Tel: 051 430 6233
Fax: 051 430 2774
E-mail: admin@ugfabrics.co.za
www.upholsteryandgeneral.co.za
Suppliers of fabrics, trimmings and tools

NEW ZEALAND

Auckland

Furniture Components (NZ) Ltd
42-46 Aintree Avenue
Mangere
Auckland
Tel: 09 275 6550

Simonson M (NZ) Ltd
Showroom – 63 Allens Road
East Tamaki
Auckland
Tel: 09 274 0321

Wellington

Affordable Upholstery
35 Waione Street
Petone
Wellington
Tel: 04 938 0098

That's Upholstery
Wingate Industrial Park
80-82 Eastern Hutt Road
Lower Hutt
Wellington
Tel: 04 567 0221

AUSTRALIA

Look in the phone book/local press/search the internet for local suppliers.

Lincraft
Head Office
31–33 Alfred Street
Blackburn VICTORIA 3130
Tel: 1800 640 107
General fabric supplier

Spotlight
Head Office
100 Market Street
South Melbourne VICTORIA 3205
Tel: 1300 305 405
www.spotlight.com.au
General fabric supplier

Index

antiques shops 12
arm: drop, covering of 143-4
    drop, finishing 144-6
armchair: Art Deco 100-7
    classic 108-16
arms: Art Deco armchair 105
    classic armchair 111, 113-14
    covering, on Art Deco armchair 105-6
    re-covering 94-6
auctions 13

back: Art Deco armchair 106
    re-covering 96
beading cane see cane, beading
blind stitching see stitching, blind
box cushion 82-9
buttoning: chaise longue 135, 137
    chesterfield 152-3
    deep-buttoned stool 71-3
    re-covering upholstery 93-4
buttons: general remarks on 11
    positioning of 70, 134-5, 151-2

calico: deep-buttoned stool 69
    drop-in seat 38
    general remarks on 11-12
    overstuffed seat 55-6
    pin-cushion seat 46-7
cane: attaching 103
    beading 81
    plugging 81
    whipping 18
caning 74-81
chair: overstuffed 58-67
    tub 124-31
    wing 118-23
chaise longue 132-9
chesterfield, buttoned leather 148-55
clove hitch see knots
cord: lay 11-12
    piping 11
corners, finishing off 40-1
cover, for box cushion 88-9
covering: chaise longue 139
    inside wing chair 120-1
cushion, box see box cushion
cushions, inners 30
cutting out, for box cushion 85
cutting plan see plan, cutting

deep-buttoned stool see stool, deep-buttoned
drop-arm sofa see sofa, drop-arm
drop-in seat see seat, drop-in

edge roll, stitching 22-3

fabric: applying 20-1
    chaise longue 136
    choice of 26-7
    deep-buttoned stool 71
    drop-in seat 39-41
    overstuffed chair 63-4
    overstuffed seat 56-7
    pin-cushion seat 48-9
    tub chair 128-9
fibre: stuffing drop-in seat 37
    vegetable 12
finishing, when re-covering upholstery 97
finishing off: Art Deco armchair 106-7
    box cushion 89
    chaise longue 139
    chesterfield 155
    classic armchair 115
    deep-buttoned stool 73
    drop-arm sofa 147
    overstuffed chair 65
    overstuffed seat 57
    tub chair 129-31
    wing chair 123
fleece, synthetic 11-12
furniture: stripping 14-15
    upholstered, buying 12-13

gimp pins see pins, gimp
gusset, for box cushion 87-8

hammer: magnetic tack 8, 10
hessian: Art Deco armchair 102, 104
    chesterfield 150
    deep-buttoned stool 68-9
    drop-in seat 37
    general remarks on 11-12
    overstuffed chair 62
    overstuffed seat 52-3
    pin-cushion seat 45
    tub chair 127-8
    wing chair 118-20
horsehair 12
hump, on chaise longue 136-8

join, Van Dyke 31

knots 18

making up, box cushion 84
mallet, wooden 8
measuring up: box cushion 84-5
    general remarks on 38
    re-covering upholstery 92

nails, upholstery 11, 49
needle: double-ended 8-10
    spring 8-10
netting staples see staples, netting

overstuffed chair see chair, overstuffed
overstuffed seat see seat, overstuffed

padding: deep-buttoned seat 70
    overstuffed seat 56
    pin-cushion seat 47
pin-cushion seat see seat, pin-cushion
pins, gimp 11
piping: box cushion 86
    double 25
    single 25
    overstuffed chair 64
    stitching 86
plan, cutting 29
plugging cane see cane, plugging

re-covering upholstery 90-9
regulator, stuffing 8-10, 19
roll, edge 69

scrolls: drop-arm sofa 147
    finishing 130-1, 147
    re-covering upholstery 97

seat: Art Deco armchair 106
    chesterfield, covering of 154
    classic armchair 112-13
    drop-arm sofa 144
    drop-in 34-41
    overstuffed 50-9
    pin-cushion 42-9
    re-covering 95
sewing machines 11
skewers, upholstery 10
slipknot see knots
sofa, drop-arm 140-7
springing: overstuffed chair 61-2
    wing chair 118
springs: arms of classic armchair 110
    attaching 61

checking 103
front-edge 103-4
seat of classic armchair 112
testing 60
tying 17
staples, netting 12
stitching: blind 53-4
hand 24
stool: box cushion 85
deep-buttoned 66-75
stripping: Art Deco armchair 102
cane 76
chaise longue 134
chesterfield 150
classic armchair 110
deep-buttoned stool 68
drop-arm sofa 142
overstuffed chair 60
overstuffed seat 52
pin-cushion seat 44
re-covering upholstery 92-3
tub chair 126
wing chair 118
see also furniture, stripping
stuffing: arms on classic armchair 111
Art Deco armchair 102, 105
chesterfield 150-1
deep-buttoned stool 68-9
drop-arm sofa 142-3
drop-in seat 38
drop-in seat 37-9
general remarks on 18
overstuffed chair 53
overstuffed seat 55
pin-cushion seat 46
stuffing, regulating
overstuffed seat 54
seat of classic armchair 112
tub chair 128
wing chair 119-20
stuffing regulator *see* regulator, stuffing
stuffing ties *see* ties, stuffing

tack lifter 10
tacking strip 12
tacks, upholstery 11-12
techniques, basic 14-31
ties, stuffing: general remarks on 19, 23, 37
overstuffed seat 55
pin-cushion seat 45
wing chair 120
tips: applying piping 113
buying at auctions 13

cane shrinkage 78
checking balance of work 121
checking cushion covers 88
choosing chair to re-upholster 93
dealing with short fabric 95
drop-arm mechanisms 143
finishing piping 130
identifying springed seats 36
judging stuffing for armchair arms 116
lining up calico 38
marker pens 85
neatening up cane furniture 81
positioning buttons 135, 137
safety 15
sequence of work 126
soaking cane 76
spacing for tacks and nails 45-6
spacing of springs 60
stuffing over springs 111
stuffing round buttons 154
stuffing seats 104
using buttoning twine 53
tools *see* under individual names
trench, on Art Deco armchair 104
tub chair *see* chair, tub
twine: buttoning 11
flax 11
general remarks on 12

upholstered furniture *see* furniture, upholstered
upholstery, re-covering *see* re-covering upholstery
upholstery skewers *see* skewers, upholstery

Van Dyke join *see* join, Van Dyke
vegetable fibre, for stuffing drop-in seat 37

wadding: cotton 11, 20
general remarks on 12
webbing: Art Deco armchair 102
box cushion 85
chaise longue 134
classic armchair 110
deep-buttoned stool 68
drop-arm sofa 142
drop-in seat 36
general remarks on 11-12, 16
overstuffed chair 60
pin-cushion seat 44
tub chair 126
wing chair 118
webbing stretcher 10

peg-and-slot 8-10
wing: covering 122-3
padding 121
wing chair *see* chair, wing

zip, for box cushion 97